Understanding Christianity 2

Sue Penney

Heinemann

Heinemann Educational Publishers
Halley Court, Jordan Hill, Oxford OX2 8EJ
a division of Reed Educational & Professional Publishing Ltd
OXFORD FLORENCE PRAGUE MADRID ATHENS
MELBOURNE AUCKLAND KUALA LUMPUR SINGAPORE TOKYO
IBADAN NAIROBI KAMPALA JOHANNESBURG GABORONE
PORTSMOUTH NH (USA) CHICAGO MEXICO CITY SAO PAULO

Heinemann is a registered trademark of Reed Educational & Professional Publishing Ltd.

Text © Sue Penney, 1998

First published 1998

01 00 99 98
10 9 8 7 6 5 4 3 2 1

British Library Cataloguing in Publication Data
A catalogue record for this book is available from the British Library

ISBN 0 435 36795 1

Designed and typeset by Artistix, Thame, Oxon
Illustrations by Catherine Ward
Cover design by Aricot Vert Design
Printed and bound in Spain by Mateu Cromo

Acknowledgements
The publishers would like to thank the following for permission to reproduce copyright material: The Central Board of Finance of the Church of England for the extracts from *The Alternative Service Book 1980*, copyright © The Central Board of Finance of the Church of England and reproduced by permission on pp.8, 25; Hodder & Stoughton Publishers for the extracts from *Run Baby Run*, by Nicky Cruz and Jamie Buckingham, on p.58; Lions Publishing plc for the extract from the *Lion Handbook: The History of Christianity* on p.32; Maranatha! Music for the extract from the hymn 'Father we love you', by Donna Adkins, copyright © Maranatha! Music, administered by Copycare, PO Box 77, Hailsham, BN27 3EF, used by permission on p.24; Methodist Publishing House for the extracts from *Hymns and Psalms* (1983) on pp.4, 25; Quotations from the Bible used throughout the book are taken from *The Good News Bible*, published by the Bible Society/HarperCollins Publishers Ltd, UK © American Bible Society, 1966, 1971, 1976, 1992.

The publishers would like to thank the following for permission to use photographs: Ancient Art & Architecture Collection Ltd. pp.39, 50, 51; Andes Press Agency/Carlos Reyes-Manzo pp.11, 21, 25, 27, 29, 41, 49; Heather Angel p.14; Bridgeman Art Library pp.19, 48; Bridgeman Art Library/Giraudon p.15; Bridgeman Art Library/Index p.6; J. Allan Cash Ltd. pp.18, 31 (all); CIRCA Photo Library p.22; C.M. Dixon pp.8, 32, 36, 38, 42, 44, 45, 52, 54; Empics/Andy Heading p.60; Format/Maggie Murray p.47; Carrie Grant p.61; Sally and Richard Greenhill p.17; Sonia Halliday and Laura Lushington pp.8, 14, 29, 46; Sonia Halliday Photographs pp.33, 42, 43; Sonia Halliday Photographs/F.H.C. Birch pp.9, 37; Robert Harding Picture Library pp.53, 58; Hutchison Library pp.5, 24, 55; Hutchison Library/John Fryer p.26; Hutchison Library/Jeremy A. Horner p.30; Hutchison Library/Nigel Sitwell p.36; Images Colour Library p.4; Katz Pictures/Richard Baker p.13; Magnum Photographers/Raghu Rai p.56; NHPA/Moira Savonius p.16; Popperfoto/Reuter p.57; Zev Radovan pp.12, 40; Science Photo Library/Porterfield Chickering p.10; Frank Spooner Pictures/Gamma p.23; Don Summers p.59; Zefa p.20.

Front cover photograph: Format Photographers

The publishers have made every effort to trace copyright holders. However, if any material has been incorrectly acknowledged, we would be pleased to correct this at the earliest opportunity.

Contents

Beliefs about God
1	The Holy Trinity	4
2	God the Father	6
3	God the Son	8
4	God the Holy Spirit	10

Beliefs about Jesus
5	Followers of Jesus 1	12
6	Followers of Jesus 2	14
7	Jesus' teachings 1	16
8	Jesus' teachings 2	18

The Christian Church
9	The sacraments	20
10	The Eucharist	22
11	Prayer	24
12	Pentecost	26
13	Early days	28
14	The Church takes shape	30
15	The life of St Paul	32
16	St Paul's missionary journeys 1	34
17	St Paul's missionary journeys 2	36

The Bible
18	St Paul's letters	38
19	The authority of the Bible	40
20	The Gospels	42
21	The Synoptic Gospels	44
22	The Ten Commandments	46
23	Jesus' commandments	48

Living as a Christian
24	The saints	50
25	Saints in Britain	52
26	Pilgrimage	54
27	Inspirational people 1	56
28	Inspirational people 2	58
29	Inspirational people 3	60

Map and time chart	62
Glossary	63

1 The Holy Trinity

I bind unto myself today
*The strong name of the **Trinity**,*
*By **invocation** of the same,*
The Three in One and One in Three,
Of whom all nature hath creation,
***Eternal** Father, Spirit, Word.*
*Praise to the Lord of my **salvation***
Salvation is of Christ the Lord.

These words are believed to have been written by St Patrick in the fourth century CE. The hymn from which they come is often called St Patrick's Breastplate. A breastplate was one of the most important pieces of armour that soldiers wore, because it protected their chest. Using this title for the hymn shows how important the beliefs in it are.

What is the Trinity?

Christians believe that there is only one God, but they believe that he can be experienced in three ways – God the Father, God the Son and God the Holy Spirit. This is why God is sometimes described as 'three in one and one in three'. This belief is called the Trinity ('tri' means three, as in tricycle). Many people – Christians too – find it a difficult idea to follow, but it is an important part of Christian belief.

Why do Christians believe in the Trinity?

The first Christians had to work out what they believed, and how their new beliefs matched what they already believed as Jews. As Jews, they were sure that there was only one God. But they also believed that Jesus was God.

Then there was the belief that Jesus had died as a human being, but that his power was still with them. Putting these beliefs together and trying to make sense of them was very difficult. For 300 years, important Christian thinkers discussed, debated and argued. Was Jesus really a man? Was he really God? How was he God's Son? What did this mean? How was it possible? Sometimes the discussions were over the meaning or the translation of just one word. But the questions and the answers were very important, because the whole religion depended on them. The leaders were putting into words beliefs which were the foundation of Christianity.

How can we describe the Trinity?

One of the first descriptions of the Trinity was written down by a man called Tertullian. He was a Roman and lived in the second century CE. He said that the Son and the Spirit come from God like rays of sunshine come from the sun. They are completely sun, but also completely themselves. Another description is supposed to have been used by St Patrick. He lived in Ireland, and there is a legend which says that one day he took a shamrock leaf and showed it to the people he was teaching. Just like a shamrock has three parts in one leaf, so God is three parts in one being.

Shamrock

Beliefs about God

Tertullian used the sun to help explain the Trinity

Why is the Trinity important?

Most Christians feel that without belief in the Trinity, it is not possible to make sense of what they believe about God. They believe that Jesus had the power to forgive **sins** (wrong-doing) when he was alive on earth, and that through the Holy Spirit he can still do this today. Only God has this power, because sins separate people from him. At the same time, God must be different from Jesus, or the **crucifixion** and death of Jesus would have been the crucifixion of God. The Spirit must be different, too, or Jesus' power would only be present when he had a human body. Most Christians believe that although it is complicated, the belief in the Trinity is the best way of putting these difficult ideas into words.

Summing up

Most Christians believe that there is one God who can be experienced in three ways.

Activities

A 1 What do Christians believe the three parts of the Trinity are?

2 Why were the arguments between early Church leaders so important?

B 3 Explain why belief in the Trinity is necessary for Christians.

4 Look at the photo opposite. Why do you think St Patrick used the example of a shamrock leaf to explain the Trinity?

C 5 Think about a glass of water, an ice cube and the steam from a boiling kettle. Explain why they might help you to understand the idea of three things which are the same but different.

2 God the Father

Note:
Christians have always used male titles when describing God. This does not mean that they think God is really male. It started in the days when men were seen as being more powerful than women. Most Christians today would agree that God is neither female nor male, but they still use 'he' when referring to God because it is convenient.

Why do Christians believe in God?

For most Christians, their belief in God comes from looking at what they believe he has made. There are so many amazing things in the world that they do not find it possible to believe that it all happened by chance. They believe that the fact that the world exists proves that God exists. For example, Christians might compare the human brain and a computer to show why they believe this. The best computer ever invented is nowhere near as good as a brain – but very few people would believe that the parts of a computer just happened to come together in the right way by chance. In the same way, Christians say that they cannot believe that human beings just happened by chance.

God the Father

Years ago many people had simpler beliefs than those of people today. They believed that God was like a sort of magician. They thought of God as an old man sitting above the clouds on a golden throne, watching what happened in the world, magically able to see everything. Today, ideas about God have advanced. Christians teach that God is a spirit – in other words, a power or force. They believe that God is eternal, all-powerful and present everywhere.

Christians see God the Father as a spirit who creates life and sustains it – that is, keeps it going. They believe that he cares about what he has made.

God the creator

The Bible says that God created the world in six days, and rested on the seventh day. Some Christians still believe that this is really what happened. Others believe that the world came about gradually in a process called **evolution**, in which things developed over millions of years. Many Christians today believe that we do not need to say that one of these beliefs is right and the other is wrong. They argue that it is possible to believe in evolution being started by and 'controlled' by a creator God. For these people, the story of creation in the Bible becomes picture language, used by people thousands of years ago when they did not really understand the way the world worked.

People used to think of God as an old man sitting above the clouds

Beliefs about God

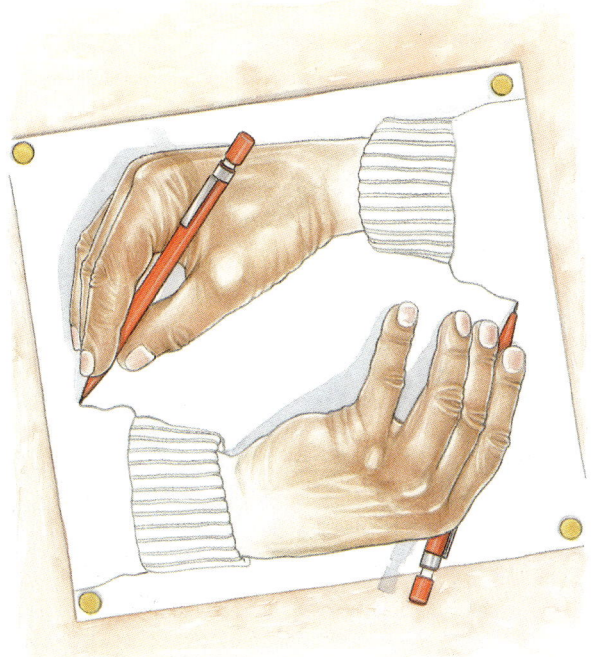

Without beginning or end...

As human beings have developed, they can accept more complicated ideas. To understand this, imagine trying to explain the rules of a complicated game to a friend of your own age. Now think of trying to explain the same thing to a child of five or six. As a person develops, they can understand more difficult explanations. Christians would say that the same is true for human beings' understanding of God.

God the carer

Christians believe that God cares about all his creation. They believe that he has a personal relationship with human beings. For Christians, this relationship is based on the belief that God made everyone and everything, and knows and cares about what he has made. This relationship is not one-sided, because Christians say that people can get to know God through prayer. This is why prayer is so important for Christians (see unit 11). They say that the proof that God cares about the world was shown best in the life of Jesus, who they believe was God the Son.

Summing up

Belief in God the Father is a basic part of Christian belief.

Activities

A 1 How would Christians back up their belief that the world could not have happened by chance?

2 Using this unit and unit 1, write down as many things as you can which Christians believe about God.

B 3 Look at the picture on this page, which shows the idea of something which never began and never ends. What Christian idea about God does this illustrate? Say whether the picture helps you to understand it.

4 Using a Bible, look up the first four verses of Psalm 19. Write a paragraph saying what you think the writer believed about God as creator.

C 5 'If God exists, he should give us some proof that he is there.' Work in pairs to think of the advantages and disadvantages of 'proof' that there is a God. What sort of proof do you think people would accept?

3 God the Son

> We believe in one Lord, Jesus Christ, the only son of God ...
> (The Nicene **Creed**)

What does being 'God's son' mean?

Christians believe that God the Son was a man called Jesus. He was a Jew who lived in a country called Palestine (modern-day Israel) in the first century CE. Christians do not believe that he was God's son in the way that the words 'father' and 'son' are usually used. They believe that God is a spirit, so it is nonsense to say that he could have a child in the usual way.

Saying that Jesus was God's Son is a sort of picture language which shows that Christians believe Jesus had a special relationship with God. They say that Jesus was unique because he was the only person who has ever lived who was totally God but also totally human. They believe that the life of Jesus shows human beings what God is really like.

This ivory statue of Mary and Jesus was carved in the twelfth century

The Church of the Annunciation in Nazareth today

Why was Jesus different?

There are some parts of Jesus' life which Christians believe show that he was unique. They believe that his conception was not the result of sexual intercourse, but was a **miracle**. (Some Christians place more emphasis than others on the belief that Jesus' mother, Mary, was a virgin.) The **Gospels** say that during his life he worked miracles. Christians believe he could have done this only if he had special power which came from God. They believe that this special power also meant that Jesus was perfect – he never sinned.

The death of Jesus

The death of Jesus and what Christians call his **Resurrection** – the belief that he came back to life after death – is the most important part of what Christians believe about Jesus. Christians believe that because Jesus was unique, his death had a unique effect on the world. They call this the **atonement**. To atone for something means to make up for something you have done wrong. Christians believe that Jesus was not making up for something he had done wrong himself, because he never sinned. They believe that he was atoning for all the sins of human beings. It is like saying that Jesus' death put human beings and God back together – 'at one' – again.

To understand how important this is, you need to understand that Christians believe that sin causes barriers between people and God. Christians say that nobody can escape sin, because no human being is perfect, so the forgiving of sins is something that changes everything. They say that it means people can have a new relationship with God. This means that death is not the end, because at the end of their life on earth they can be with God for ever. This is called eternal life. One of the most important verses in the Bible sums this up.

> 'God loved the world so much that he gave his only Son, so that everyone who believes in him may not die but have eternal life.'
> (John 3, 16)

Christians believe that Jesus' death was very important

The Resurrection and Ascension

Christians believe that Jesus died when he was crucified on Good Friday, but that two days later, on Easter Sunday, he came back to life again. Different Christians have different views about what actually happened at the Resurrection, but most would agree that nothing like it has ever happened before or since. In the six weeks after the Resurrection, they believe that Jesus' **disciples** saw him several times. Christians believe that they saw him for the last time at the **Ascension**, when he promised his disciples that he would send them a 'helper'. Christians call this helper the Holy Spirit.

Summing up

Christians believe that Jesus' special relationship with God means he should be called God's Son.

Activities

A 1 In what ways do Christians believe that Jesus is unique?

2 Why might Christians have differing views about what happened at the Resurrection?

B 3 Explain what Christians mean when they say that Jesus is God's Son.

4 Why is the idea of forgiveness of sins so important in Christianity? In pairs, think of examples of the sort of things which might put up barriers between people and God.

C 5 In your own words, explain what 'atonement' means. Then write a short story in which someone makes up for something that they have done wrong.

4 God the Holy Spirit

What is the Holy Spirit?

Christians believe that the Holy Spirit is the third part of the Trinity, the power of God working in the world. They believe that Jesus promised this power to his disciples before he left them. In John's Gospel, Jesus tells his disciples that he will ask God to give them, 'another Helper, who will stay with you for ever.' Jesus described this Helper as, 'the Spirit who reveals the truth about God.' (John 14, 16).

In the book called the Acts of the Apostles, Jesus says this to his disciples just before the Ascension:

> 'Do not leave Jerusalem, but wait for the gift I told you about, the gift my Father promised. John baptized with water, but in a few days you will be baptized with the Holy Spirit.'
>
> 'When the Holy Spirit comes upon you, you will be filled with power and you will be witnesses for me in Jerusalem, in all Judaea and Samaria, and to the ends of the earth.'
>
> (Acts 1, 5, 8)

Christians say that this **baptism** with the Holy Spirit took place at Pentecost (see unit 12).

The gifts of the Spirit

Christians believe that the Holy Spirit gives special powers. An early Christian teacher, called St Paul (see unit 15), wrote letters to Christian friends. Some of them are included in the Bible, and in one of them he said:

> *The Spirit gives one person the power to work miracles; to another, the gift of speaking God's message; and to yet another, the ability to tell the difference between gifts that come from the Spirit and those that do not. To one person he gives the ability to speak in strange tongues, and to another he gives the ability to explain what is said ... as he wishes, he gives a different gift to each person.*
>
> (I Corinthians 12, 10–11)

Christians believe that the Holy Spirit has always been at work in the world. Most Christians today would say that there are times when they are aware of God working in their lives, and they believe that this is the power of God's Spirit. Some Christians believe that this power can be seen directly. Others feel that the Spirit can work through the words of the Bible or of a Christian preacher or teacher.

Some powers can only be seen by what they do

Beliefs about God

Being filled with the Spirit

Experience of the Spirit

Christians who teach that the Spirit can be seen working directly often belong to the groups of Churches called **Pentecostal** or **Charismatic**. They speak of people being 'filled with the Spirit' and believe that when this happens the person may possess the special powers given by the Spirit. For example, they believe that the person may be able to preach to others or be given power to heal people who are ill. Their worship may include people 'speaking in tongues'. This is when someone begins to speak, but usually their words are not recognizable in any language. The person often experiences great joy and a feeling that they are being 'given' the words they are saying. It is seen as a special way of worshipping.

Christians who do not have the same belief in the power of the Spirit being seen directly still believe that the Spirit is very important. They believe that through the power of the Spirit people can understand more about God, especially in the life of Jesus and through reading the Bible and worshipping together. Many Christians believe that the Spirit guides people, and is a source of love and joy in people's lives.

Summing up

For Christians, the Holy Spirit is the way God works in the world.

Activities

A 1 What are the main ways in which Christians believe God's Spirit can be seen in the world?

2 Look again at the passage from I Corinthians. Make a list of the 'gifts of the Spirit', using your own words.

B 3 Why do you think some Christians pray to be 'filled with the Spirit'?

4 The word that is usually translated as 'spirit' can also be translated as 'breath' or 'wind'. Using the picture opposite to give you ideas, think of as many reasons as you can for Christians saying that the Spirit is like forces in nature.

C 5 If possible, try to arrange for a visitor from a Pentecostal or Charismatic Church to come to talk to your group. Prepare some questions to ask them about how they worship. If you cannot arrange for someone to come, you may be able to watch a video of a service where Christians are worshipping in this way.

5 Followers of Jesus 1

Many religious teachers have followers who spend time listening to them teach and trying to learn from them. Teachers often encourage this, because it is one way in which their teachings can be remembered when they are no longer there. In Jesus' time, many people could not read, and there were no newspapers or radio and television, so people learned things by heart. Teachers made their words easy to remember by telling stories and by using speech patterns where phrases were repeated so they stayed in the memory.

Who were Jesus' followers?

Jesus' followers were ordinary men and women who were so impressed with his teaching that they chose to spend time with him. It is a mistake to think that all Jesus' followers gave up their ordinary lives. Some probably did, but others would have come and gone as their jobs and families allowed. Jesus' closest followers are usually called his disciples.

What is a disciple?

The word disciple means someone who learns. In this sense, everyone who went to listen to Jesus preaching was a disciple, but when Christians talk about Jesus' disciples, they usually mean one of the twelve special followers who were with Jesus for most of the three years when he was preaching and teaching.

The chosen twelve

The list of the twelve disciples is more or less the same in each of the first three Gospels. This is Mark's version.

Jesus did much of his teaching in Galilee – this is what it looks like today

> *Then Jesus went up a hill and called to himself the men he wanted. They came to him, and he chose twelve, whom he named* **apostles**. *'I have chosen you to be with me,' he told them. 'I will also send you out to preach, and you will have authority to drive out demons.' These are the twelve he chose: Simon (Jesus gave him the name Peter); James and his brother John, the sons of Zebedee (Jesus gave them the name Boanerges, which means 'Men of Thunder'); Andrew, Philip, Bartholomew, Matthew, Thomas, James son of Alphaeus, Thaddaeus, Simon the Patriot and Judas Iscariot, who betrayed Jesus.*
>
> (Mark 3, 13–19)

Beliefs about Jesus

All the Gospels say that the two sets of brothers, Simon and Andrew, and James and John, were the first disciples. Jesus gave Simon the name Peter, which means rock. Peter, James and John were probably the ones who were closest to Jesus during his ministry. The story of how Jesus asked them to be his followers is in the first chapter of Mark's Gospel, and the fourth chapters of the Gospels of Matthew and Luke.

Matthew

Matthew is the only other disciple whose 'call' is described in detail. The first three Gospels all say that Matthew (also called Levi, his Jewish name) was working as a tax-collector when Jesus called to him to follow him. He got up, left his office and became a disciple. The fact that he was a tax-collector was very important, because in those days Jews hated tax-collectors. By choosing a tax-collector to be one of his friends, Jesus was showing that his teaching was for everyone, not just the religious people in society.

Judas Iscariot

Wherever he is mentioned in the Gospels, Judas' name is followed by the words 'who betrayed Jesus'. Judas was the disciple who told the authorities where Jesus could be found on the night that he was arrested. Christians have always wondered why Judas did this. Some people think he did it for money, as the authorities paid him for the information. Others think that he believed Jesus needed to be forced to show his power. Perhaps Judas felt that having Jesus arrested would do this. It seems certain that Judas did not intend what happened – Matthew's Gospel says that after the crucifixion he returned the money and then committed suicide.

Summing up

Jesus needed followers to pass on his teaching.

Billy Graham, a twentieth century Christian preacher

Activities

A
1. What does the name 'Peter' mean? What do you think Jesus was saying when he gave Simon this name?

2. What does the nickname 'men of thunder' tell you about the characters of James and John?

B
3. Why was it important that Jesus chose Matthew to be a disciple? Write about what you think Matthew's feelings were.

4. What do you think the Gospel-writers felt about Judas Iscariot? How can you tell?

C
5. When a religious leader today wants lots of people to hear and remember their teaching, what methods can they use? Which methods do you think are the most effective?

6 Followers of Jesus 2

There are several places in the Gospels where the writers tell the story of how they believe Jesus changed someone's life. This unit looks at two of these stories.

Zacchaeus

Like the disciple Matthew, Zacchaeus was a tax-collector. At the time of Jesus, Jews hated the tax-collectors, who worked for the Romans. As well as being the enemy power who had taken over the Jews' country, the Romans were **Gentiles** (non-Jews). At this time, no good Jew would have anything to do with a Gentile. By taking a job which involved contact with Gentiles, tax-collectors were breaking the laws of their religion. It was also well known that the Romans did not ask questions about how much money was collected so long as they got their tax. The tax-collectors were believed to be cheats who took extra for themselves.

Zacchaeus lived in Jericho, and Luke's Gospel says that 'he was rich'. When Jesus came to Jericho, Zacchaeus had evidently heard of him, and he wanted to see the man who the crowds were gathering to look at.

However, Zacchaeus was not very tall, and the crowd was so great that he could not see. He decided to climb a tree which he knew was on the route that Jesus would follow. When Jesus came there, he looked up and said to Zacchaeus, 'Hurry down, because I must stay in your house today'. The crowd began grumbling that Jesus was mixing with a man who had done wrong, but Zacchaeus stood up and announced that he would give half of everything he owned to the poor, and repay – four times over – anyone he had cheated.

A Roman coin from the time of the Emperor Claudius (41-54 CE)

Luke says that Zacchaeus climbed a sycamore tree, perhaps like this one

Jesus used the opportunity to tell the crowd what he had said before – 'The Son of Man [a title he often used for himself] came to seek and to save the lost.'

Mary Magdalene

Mary Magdalene's name occurs several times in the Gospels. In Luke's Gospel she is described as a woman 'from whom seven demons had been driven out' (Luke 8, 2). This may be picture language for some form of mental illness. Luke wanted to make it clear that Mary was someone whom Jesus had healed.

Although she was not one of the twelve disciples, Mary obviously became a close follower, and she is mentioned several times in the story of the Resurrection. She was one of the women who went to the tomb where Jesus had been buried, to **anoint** his body with oil and spices. In John's Gospel, she was the first follower to see Jesus after the Resurrection.

In this story, she was weeping in the Garden of Gethsemane because she thought someone had taken Jesus' body away. When Jesus appeared in front of her she did not recognize him, and thought he was the gardener. It was not until he called her name that she realized who he was, and then Jesus told her to go and tell the other disciples that he had risen.

There are very few details in the Gospels about Mary's life, but the people for whom the Gospels were written probably knew much more about her. The writers wanted to show how knowing Jesus changed her from a woman who needed healing into someone who was one of Jesus' closest friends.

Why are these stories important?

The Gospel writers used stories like these to show the effect that Jesus could have on people. They were sure that Jesus' message was for everyone. By using stories of how Jesus changed ordinary people like Zacchaeus and Mary, they were showing that Jesus' message was for other ordinary people, too.

Part of a fifteenth century painting showing Mary Magdelene washing Jesus' feet

Beliefs about Jesus

Summing up

The Gospel writers wanted to show that Jesus attracted ordinary people to follow him.

Activities

A 1 At the time of Jesus why did Jews try to avoid contact with tax-collectors?

2 Why do you think the Gospel writers emphasized that Jesus had healed Mary?

B 3 What did Jesus mean when he talked about Zacchaeus being 'lost'?

4 The Gospels show that Mary cared very much for Jesus. Why do you think she was upset when she thought that Jesus' body had been taken away?

C 5 Imagine that you were a newspaper reporter at the time of Jesus. You hear unbelievable reports about Zacchaeus, who was well known and very disliked in the town of Jericho. Write a report for your newspaper about what has happened. (It may help you to look up the story in the Bible, Luke 19, 1–10.)

7 Jesus' teachings 1

The Kingdom of God

A large part of Jesus' teaching is about the Kingdom of God. Mark's Gospel says that the first thing Jesus said when he began preaching was, 'The right time has come – the Kingdom of God is near.' To understand Jesus' teaching, it is important to understand what he meant when he talked about the Kingdom of God.

What is the Kingdom of God?

People who have studied the Bible agree that when Jesus talked about the Kingdom of God, he was talking about something happening, rather than a place or a country. He talked about it in lots of different ways – as something that was coming, as something that was already here, as something which would show God's power, as something that could only be understood by someone who had the attitude of a child. He told lots of **parables** (teaching stories) about it. The idea behind all of his teaching about the Kingdom of God is that God is in charge of the world. People may ignore him and go their own way, but one day God will prove that he really is the ruler. Christians say that Jesus' teaching can be summed up in the idea that the Kingdom of God is everything that God wants to do in the world. For Christians, this can happen through the life and work of Jesus.

The parable of the mustard seed

This parable is one of many which Jesus told about the Kingdom of God.

> 'What shall we say the Kingdom of God is like?... It is like this. A man takes a mustard seed, the smallest seed in the world, and plants it in the ground. After a while it grows up and becomes the biggest of all plants. It puts out such large branches that the birds come and make their nests in its shade.'
>
> (Mark 4, 30–32)

Christians say that in this parable, Jesus was showing how powerful the Kingdom of God is. Just like a tiny mustard seed grows into a huge plant, the Kingdom of God grows, little by little, but eventually its effect will be seen. Because of the lesson it teaches, the parable is a favourite one for many Christians. They believe that it shows how even one person's efforts to do something good can lead to results which are much greater than they could hope for.

A tiny mustard seed becomes a large plant

Beliefs about Jesus

Jesus blesses little children

Some people brought small children to Jesus for him to place his hands on them. They did this to show their respect for Jesus and because they hoped that it would result in blessings for their children. When the disciples saw them, they shouted at the people and told them to go away, probably because they felt that Jesus was tired and would not want to be bothered with the children. Jesus called the children to him and said:

> '*Let the children come to me and do not stop them, because the Kingdom of God belongs to such as these. Remember this! Whoever does not receive the Kingdom of God like a child will never enter it.*'
>
> (Luke 18, 15–17)

Christians have used this story to show Jesus' kindness, but they believe it also shows that Jesus was encouraging his followers to have the openness and honesty of a small child. They believe he was saying that God's Kingdom is available for everyone, but that anyone who tries to be grand and important is missing the point. He was saying that people need to depend on God in the same way that a small child depends on his or her parents.

'The Kingdom of God belongs to such as these'

Summing up

Christians believe that the things Jesus taught about the Kingdom of God are some of the most important parts of his teaching.

Activities

A 1 Look carefully at the description of the mustard seed in the parable and the picture opposite. Why do you think Jesus chose this particular seed for his story?

  2 Why is someone who tries to be important missing the point of Jesus' teaching about the Kingdom of God?

B 3 How might Christians use the idea behind Jesus' teaching about God's Kingdom to explain things that are wrong with the world today?

  4 Why were the parents bringing their children to Jesus? Can you think of any examples of people today whom parents might want to bring their children to see?

C 5 Christians say that one of the lessons of the parable of the mustard seed is that you should do your best, even if you think your efforts are not worth much. Explain why this is a lesson of the story. Then write a story of your own which shows how a small action can have a great effect.

8 Jesus' teachings 2

The Lord's Prayer

'When you pray, do not use a lot of meaningless words, as the pagans do, who think that their gods will hear them because their prayers are long. Do not be like them. Your Father already knows what you need before you ask him. This, then, is how you should pray:

Our Father in heaven:
May your holy name be honoured;
may your Kingdom come;
may your will be done on earth as it is in heaven.
Give us today the food we need.
Forgive us the wrongs we have done, as we forgive the wrongs that others have done to us.
Do not bring us to hard testing, but keep us safe from the Evil One.'

(Matthew 6, 7–13)

This was the prayer that Jesus taught his disciples. Because they often call Jesus 'Lord', Christians call it the Lord's Prayer. It is used more often than any other prayer, and many Christians use it as a pattern or model for other prayers. The version here comes from a modern translation of the Bible. The words that are normally used in worship come from a translation made hundreds of years ago. Whole books have been written about why Jesus used particular words and what he meant. This section looks at some of the teachings in the Lord's Prayer which Christians think are most important.

Our Father

At the time of Jesus, Jews were used to the idea of God as a Father. What makes this prayer different is the word that Jesus used. He spoke the **Aramaic** language, and used the word **'abba'**. This is best translated as 'daddy'. It suggested a much closer relationship with God than anything that the Jews normally used at the time. Christians also believe it is important that Jesus said 'Our' Father – in other words, anyone who was a follower of his could claim this special relationship with God.

May your Kingdom come

The idea of God's Kingdom being set up on earth is part of what Jesus was teaching all the way through the Gospels. Here Jesus is saying that setting up God's Kingdom and people obeying God go together.

This church is built on the hill where Jesus is supposed to have taught his disciples

Beliefs about Jesus

A thirteenth century painting of Jesus teaching his disciples

Give us today the food we need

The point of this sentence is about trust in God. Jesus was telling his followers to pray only for what they needed, not for everything they could want. They are also to pray only for what they need at the moment. They should trust God for the future.

Forgive us the wrongs we have done

This was something quite different from Jewish teaching at the time. Everyone believed that they needed God to forgive them for the things they had done wrong. But Jesus was saying that his followers could only ask for as much forgiveness from God as they were prepared to give people who had done wrong to them.

Do not bring us to hard testing

The people listening to Jesus were used to the idea of being tested by God to see what sort of people they were. This was a prayer that when hard times came, they should not fail the test.

Keep us safe from the Evil One

At the time of Jesus, the usual idea of evil was as a devil-person. Some people still believe this today. Other people believe in an evil power which is the opposite of God. The prayer is about keeping away from evil, however it appears.

Summing up

Christians believe that the Lord's Prayer contains important Christian teachings.

Activities

A 1 Explain why Christians believe that the Lord's Prayer is the most important prayer they know.

2 What do you think is the difference between describing God as 'daddy' and as 'father'?

B 3 Why do you think Jesus told his followers they should only pray about things they needed now, rather than for the future? What do you think about this?

4 What sorts of testing can you think of that would show what sort of a person you are? (You could discuss this in pairs or small groups.)

C 5 Write a short story about somebody who needs to be forgiven for something they have done wrong. Look at newspapers or TV news programmes for ideas.

9 The sacraments

The word **sacrament** comes from a Latin word which means to make something holy. In most Churches it is the name given to the most important services. Many Christians believe that the sacraments are a special way in which they can receive God's blessing in their lives. A sacramental service includes something that can be seen, which is a **symbol** for something which cannot be seen.

The Roman Catholic and Orthodox Churches

The **Roman Catholic** and **Orthodox** Churches use seven sacraments. These are:

- baptism
- **confirmation** (**chrismation** in the Orthodox Churches)
- the **Eucharist** (sometimes called Holy Communion)
- **confession**
- **ordination**
- marriage
- anointing the sick.

A baby being baptized in an Orthodox church

Baptism and confirmation

At baptism a person has water poured on them or is immersed in water as a sign that their sins are being taken away. At confirmation the person confirms ('makes again') the promises made at their baptism. In the Orthodox Churches, the equivalent of confirmation is chrismation. It follows immediately after baptism, and the person is anointed with oil as a sign that they are receiving the Holy Spirit.

The Eucharist

The Eucharist is the service in which Christians eat bread and drink wine as a reminder of the last meal that Jesus ate with his disciples. (This is described in the next unit.)

Confession

In confession, a person tells a priest the things they have done wrong. They promise that they are really sorry. Then the priest 'speaks for' God, telling the person that their sins have been forgiven.

Ordination

Ordination is the service where a man or woman is made a member of the clergy (a vicar, priest or minister). When a person is ordained, a senior member of the clergy lays their hands on the person's head. This is a sign to show God's blessing, and to show that the person has been set apart to do God's work.

Marriage

In the sacrament of marriage, a man and woman promise that they will live together and love each other until one of them dies. The sign of this is the giving and receiving of a ring or rings. In the Orthodox Churches, the couple wear crowns for part of the ceremony as another outward sign.

The Christian Church

Laying hands on the person's head is an important part of an ordination service

Anointing the sick

When someone is very ill or very old, they may be anointed with oil. This is a sign of healing. However, it does not mean the person is always expected to get better – the anointing may be a sign of healing for the soul, a preparation for death.

The Protestant Churches

Most **Protestants** accept only two sacraments (baptism and the Eucharist) because they believe these are the only two in which Jesus took part. Most Churches hold at least some of the other services, but they do not regard them as being sacraments.

The Salvation Army, the Society of Friends and some Evangelical Churches do not accept any of the sacraments. This is because they do not believe that God is especially present at some services. They believe that God is equally present all the time.

Summing up

For many Christians, sacraments are ways in which they believe they can become especially close to God.

Activities

A 1 What do many Christians believe about the sacraments?

2 Which Churches accept only two sacraments? Why do they think these are the most important?

B 3 Sacraments have been called 'an act of the body which has a meaning for the soul'. Explain what you think this means.

4 Write a short paragraph about each of the seven sacraments, explaining what happens in each one and what it symbolizes.

C 5 'Tea and biscuits shared with love can be just as much a sacrament as bread and wine.' This was said by a member of the Society of Friends. What do you think he meant? Why would some Christians not agree with him?

10 The Eucharist

> Here Lord, we take the broken bread
> And drink the wine, believing
> That by your life our souls are fed,
> Your parting gifts receiving.
> As you have giv'n so we would give
> Ourselves for others healing;
> As you have lived so we would live
> The Father's love revealing.

Eucharist comes from a Greek word which means thanksgiving. For most Christians the service of the Eucharist is the most important part of church worship. It has several other names which are used in different Churches – Mass, Holy Communion, the Lord's Supper, the Breaking of Bread. Whatever it is called, the service celebrates the last meal that Jesus ate with his disciples. This is the meal that Christians usually call the Last Supper, when Jesus took bread and wine and gave it to his disciples as a symbol that he was going to die. At the Eucharist, Christians thank God that they can worship him, and for what they believe Jesus' death did for the world.

Teaching about the Eucharist has been an important part of Christianity since its beginning. When St Paul was writing to his friends in Corinth, he included a description of the Last Supper which was obviously well known in the Church at the time.

> For I received from the Lord the teaching that I passed on to you: that the Lord Jesus, on the night he was betrayed, took a piece of bread, gave thanks to God, broke it, and said, 'This is my body, which is for you. Do this in memory of me.' In the same way, after the supper he took the cup and said, 'This cup is God's new covenant, sealed with my blood. Whenever you drink it, do so in memory of me.' This means that every time you eat this bread and drink from this cup you proclaim the Lord's death until he comes.
>
> (I Corinthians 11, 23–26)

Descriptions of Eucharist services which date back to the very early days of Christianity, show that the service has changed very little. A typical service begins with prayers that praise God and thank him that people can worship him. The people repeat their beliefs about God and Jesus, often in the words of one of the creeds, the statements of Christian belief which have been used for hundreds of years. Then they receive a small piece of bread and a sip of wine. The bread and wine have been specially blessed. Christians believe that this blessing is very important, because it makes the bread and wine a 'spiritual food'. The service ends with everyone thanking God for his goodness and asking for his help in their lives.

A Eucharist service in an Anglican church

The Christian Church

An open-air Eucharist during a visit to Berlin by Pope John Paul II

Although the basic service is the same, there are some differences in the way the various Churches celebrate it. In Roman Catholic and some **Anglican** Churches, for example, small, round wafers are used rather than bread. In many **Free Churches**, individual glasses are used rather than a **chalice** – the large cup from which everyone drinks in Roman Catholic and Anglican services. These glasses often contain a special non-alcoholic wine or fruit juice rather than the wine used in other Churches. In some Free Churches, the people may also stay in their seats rather than going forward to kneel at the front of the church. In Orthodox Churches, the people are given the bread and wine together on a spoon, and they will all have **fasted** (gone without food and drink) before the service. Some other Christians fast too, because they believe that the bread and wine are so special that they should prepare themselves before they go to the service.

Summing up

For most Christians, the bread and wine of the Eucharist service have a special importance.

Activities

A 1 Why did Jesus give his disciples bread and wine at the Last Supper?

2 Why do you think the service is celebrated in slightly different ways in different Churches?

B 3 What do you think Christians mean when they call the bread and wine 'spiritual food'?

4 What difference do you think it makes when Christians fast before they go to a Eucharist service?

C 5 Look at the hymn at the start of the unit. Write your own hymn or poem which describes what Christians feel about the Eucharist service.

11 Prayer

Prayer is important to followers of all religions. When Jesus taught his disciples how to pray (see unit 8) he said 'When you pray' – he did not say '*If you pray.*'

What is prayer?

Many people think that prayer means asking God for what you want. The other half of this idea is that God should give people whatever they ask for when they pray to him. Christians believe that prayer is much more than this. They believe that as the creator, God knows what people need better than they know themselves, and prayer is not an automatic short-cut to receiving good things. They say that God gives people what they need, which is not always what they want. If God was a magician who made all your dreams come true when you asked him, being a Christian could be a passport to winning the lottery or never being ill!

Christians think of prayer as being like a conversation with God. They say that prayer is not just the time to tell God what you want.

It is the time to find out what God has planned for you, and to find out what he wants for your life. In the teachings of Christianity, listening to God is just as important a part of prayer as talking to him. For Christians this answers the question many people ask, which is 'What is the point of praying to God if he knows everything?'.

How do Christians pray?

There are many different sorts of prayer. Christians teach that the most important prayers come into one of four main groups.

Adoration

Adoration means deep love, so a prayer of adoration shows how much you love God. An example of this sort of prayer is often sung as a modern hymn:

> *Father we love you,*
> *we worship and adore you,*
> *Glorify your name in all the earth.*

Confession

In prayers of confession, Christians tell God the things they have done wrong, and say that they are sorry. This is part of a prayer used in the Eucharist service in many Churches:

> *Almighty God, our heavenly Father,*
> *we have sinned against you and*
> *against our fellow men,*
> *in thought and word and deed,*
> *in the evil we have done,*
> *in the good we have not done ...*
> *We are truly sorry and **repent** of all*
> *our sins ...*

Prayer can be quiet and thoughtful ...

... or loud and joyful!

Thanksgiving

This kind of prayer is to thank God for all the things that Christians believe he has done for them. A hymn which was written 500 years ago says:

> Now thank we all our God,
> with hearts and hands and voices,
> Who wondrous things has done,
> in whom his world rejoices.
> Who from our mothers' arms
> has blessed us on our way
> With countless gifts of love,
> and still is ours today.

Intercession

Intercession means asking for something on behalf of someone else. Christians often use this sort of prayer. They pray for people they know, for people who are ill, for leaders of the country, etc. In church services, intercessions are usually groups of very short prayers. They often follow a pattern where each group ends with the vicar or leader of the service saying 'Lord, in your mercy' and the people join in, saying 'Hear our prayer'.

Summing up

Christians believe that prayer is a way of communicating with God.

Activities

A 1 Why should prayer be important to followers of all religions?

2 Why do Christians believe that prayer is like a conversation?

B 3 What reasons do Christians give why God sometimes seems not to answer prayers? What do you think about this?

4 Write down as many reasons as you can why Christians think that it is important to pray for other people as well as themselves.

C 5 In the teachings of Christianity, listening to God is important. Write down as many ways as you can think of in which God could communicate with someone. Work in small groups to discuss what you think would be the best way.

12 Pentecost

The story of the early days of Christianity is found in the Acts of the Apostles, which was written by Luke. Luke writes that after the Ascension of Jesus, the disciples returned to Jerusalem, to wait for the 'helper' which Jesus had promised them. He makes it clear that they still did not really understand what was happening. They believed that Jesus was alive, but they were still afraid of the Jewish authorities, and they thought that as Jesus' friends they could be in danger themselves. There is no record of how many people were followers of Jesus at this time, but in one part of the story Luke says that there were 120 people gathered together.

The giving of the Holy Spirit

According to Luke's account, 'all the believers' – he does not say how many – were together. They may have been hiding to keep out of the way of the Jewish authorities. It was the day of the Jewish festival of Pentecost. This takes place seven weeks after the festival of Passover, the time when Jesus had been crucified. Luke says that the followers heard a noise which sounded like a rushing wind filling the house, and they saw what looked like tongues of flame which touched each person there. They forgot that they were afraid, and rushed outside. They began speaking in different languages, and soon attracted the attention of a large crowd of people. Some of the crowd decided that the men were drunk, but Peter said that this was not true. He began telling the crowd what they believed about Jesus and the work he had done. Luke says that on that day, 3000 people became followers of Jesus.

What do Christians believe happened at Pentecost?

Many Christians believe that the story of Pentecost in the Acts of the Apostles is a straightforward account of the events that happened. Other Christians believe that the account includes some picture language.

A Whit Sunday procession in Manchester

The Christian Church

Red altar cloths are used for Pentecost, to remind people that the Holy Spirit came like fire

For example, they point out that the power of God is often described as fire or wind in the Jewish **Scriptures**, and this may be why Luke used that description. Many Christians believe that the disciples really talked in foreign languages which the people listening could understand. Other Christians prefer to think that the disciples were excited, and it was their excitement which the crowd understood, rather than the exact words.

Whatever they believe about what happened, all Christians agree that the important thing about Pentecost was the effect that it had on the followers. They had been men and women who were in hiding, afraid that they were going to be killed. They were changed into people who were prepared to go out and tell anyone who wanted to listen about what they believed.

The birthday of the Church

Because they believe that the events of Pentecost were so important, many Christians think of it as being the real beginning of the Christian Church. Christians still celebrate it every year on the day which is also called Whit Sunday. There are special church services, and in many places Christians go on processions through the local area as a way of showing what they believe. This reminds everyone that Christians believe that the Holy Spirit who was given to the first disciples at Pentecost is still working in the world today.

Summing up

Pentecost celebrations mark the time when the Christian Church really began.

Activities

A 1 Why do you think the power of God is described as being like wind and fire?

2 Explain why many Christians think of Pentecost as the real beginning of the Christian Church.

B 3 Whit Sunday used to be a very popular day for people to be baptized or confirmed. Why do you think this was so?

4 In what ways would Christians today say that the Holy Spirit is working in the world?

C 5 In pairs, hold a conversation that two of the disciples might have had on the evening of the day of Pentecost. How do you think they would have been feeling? What might they be planning to do next? Listen to the conversations of other pairs in your group.

13 Early days

Jesus and all the early disciples were Jews. Jews at that time were waiting for God to send a **Messiah** who would free them from the Romans and begin God's Kingdom on earth. For some time after Jesus' death and Resurrection, his followers were Jews who believed that Jesus was this Messiah. They probably had no intention of starting a new religion. At the time many other groups in **Judaism** followed individuals who had taught a particular message.

Gradually, it became clear that the followers of Jesus were different from other Jews. They lived together as a community, sharing all their possessions equally. Luke says that:

> *All the believers continued together in close fellowship and shared their belongings with one another. They would sell their property and possessions, and distribute the money among all, according to what each one needed. Day after day they met as a group in the **Temple**, and they had their meals together in their homes, eating with glad and humble hearts, praising God, and enjoying the good will of all the people.*
>
> (Acts 2, 44–47)

They were called 'Followers of the Way', because they followed the way that Jesus had taught. But they were following a man who had been crucified. To Jews, crucifixion was the most shameful death possible. Jewish leaders were angry at the message the Followers were teaching, because they felt it was impossible that God's Messiah could have died such a death. To claim that God had resurrected him was **blasphemy**.

The first miracle

Matters came to a head one afternoon when Peter and John were going to the Temple. Outside the Beautiful Gate, which was one of the entrances to the Temple, sat a man who had been lame all his life. In those days there were no pensions or allowances for people who could not work. If someone was disabled and did not have a family to look after them they either begged or they starved. This man had friends who carried him to the Temple every day, so that he could beg from the crowds who were going to worship.

> *The beggar asked Peter and John for money, but Peter said, "'I have no money at all, but I give you what I have: in the name of Jesus Christ of Nazareth, I order you to get up and walk!'" He pulled the man to his feet, and 'at once the man's feet and ankles became strong ... he went into the Temple with them, walking and jumping and praising God.'*
>
> (Acts 3, 6–8).

The man must have been well known, and a crowd soon gathered when people saw him walking around. Peter used the opportunity to tell everyone again what the disciples believed – that Jesus had been killed but God had brought him back to life and it was through his power that the man had been cured. 'It was faith in Jesus that has made him well,' he said.

The Christian Church

This stained glass window in Lichfield Cathedral shows Peter and John healing the beggar

The authorities heard what Peter was saying, and sent for the two disciples. Luke says 'there was nothing they could say, because the man who had been healed was standing there'. They sent Peter and John away, telling them that they must not preach about Jesus any more. The two disciples went back to their friends, but they did not do as the Jewish leaders had told them to. They continued preaching about Jesus, and more and more people became Christians.

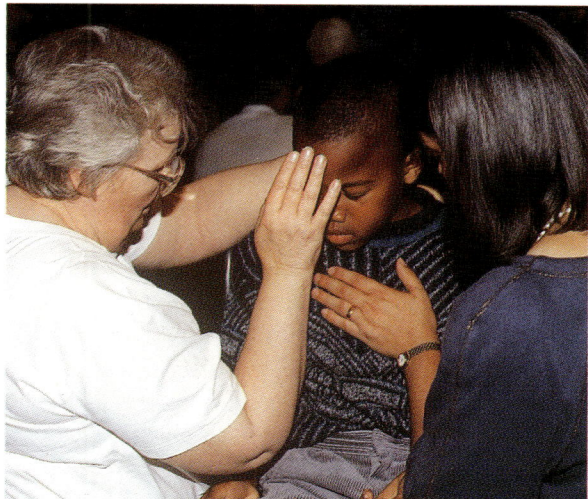

Christians believe that God still heals people today

Summing up

In the early days of Christianity, many people became Christians even though the Jewish leaders did not approve of the teaching.

Activities

A 1 Think of as many reasons as you can why the Jews found it hard to believe that Jesus was the Messiah.

2 Why would the entrance to the Temple have been a good place for the lame man to beg?

B 3 Why do you think the Christians put all their possessions together and lived as one community? What are the disadvantages and advantages of living like this?

4 Why do you think that Peter and John did not do what the Jewish authorities told them to? What reasons do you think they would give? Is it always wrong not to do as you are told?

C 5 Write the diary entry which the lame man might have made that night. How do you think he felt?

14 The Church takes shape

As news about Jesus spread, more and more people became interested in the new beliefs. As the number of followers increased, it became more difficult for them to remain a part of Judaism. Whilst all the followers were Jews, there were no problems in living as Jews and keeping the Jewish laws. But when people who were not Jews wanted to become followers, too, it began to cause difficulties.

Jews at the time did not mix with Gentiles. Especially, they did not eat with them. Followers of Jesus shared a special meal of bread and wine. How could they eat this together if some followers were not Jews? To do so meant breaking the strict rules which are an essential part of being a Jew.

One possible answer to this problem was that anyone who wanted to become a follower of Jesus had to become a Jew first. This would have meant that they had to obey all the laws of the Jewish faith. It seems that some Christians felt that this was the only answer. Others felt that it was unfair to expect anyone who had not been brought up as a Jew to become one.

Peter's vision

Peter was one of the leaders of the early Christians, and the problem of Gentile followers must have been something he spent a lot of time thinking about. He was visiting Christians in Joppa (modern-day Jaffa) when he had a **vision**. He saw a huge piece of cloth being let down from the sky. It was full of animals, reptiles and birds. A voice told him to get up, kill and eat. The Jewish laws about food meant that Peter would have been breaking the laws of Judaism if he had eaten them. He said that he could not possibly do this. The voice told him that God had made everything in the sheet, and it was not for him to say what was fit to eat or not. This happened three times.

In those days, people were sure that visions like this contained messages from God. As Peter was trying to work out what this vision meant, a messenger arrived from a Roman soldier called Cornelius. Although Cornelius was a Roman and therefore a Gentile, he was very interested in the Jewish religion. The messengers said that Cornelius, too, had had a vision, in which he had been told to talk to Peter. Peter realized that the two visions were connected. Just as the voice had told him that it was not for him to judge which of the animals on the sheet he could eat, so it was not for him to judge who could be told about Jesus.

Peter went with the messengers to Cornelius' house, and told him what had happened. Then he preached to him and his family about Jesus. The Bible says that, whilst he was speaking, 'the Holy Spirit came down on all those who were listening'. This convinced Peter that he was right to preach to Gentiles.

The port and old town of Jaffa today

These are some of the animals which Jews are forbidden to eat

The Council of Jerusalem

From this time on, Peter became convinced that it was right for non-Jews to be told the message of Jesus. There were still many people among the early Christians who did not agree. To try to sort out the disagreement, a meeting of all the Christian leaders was held in Jerusalem. This meeting is called the Council of Jerusalem.

The leaders listened to the evidence from people who had worked among the Gentiles, and they agreed that it was God's will that Gentiles should become Christians. Some basic rules were made for everyone to keep so that some of the most important laws of Judaism were not broken. They were not to eat anything which had been offered to an **idol** (false god), not to eat anything with blood in it or an animal that had been strangled, and they must live moral lives. If they did this, it was agreed that Gentiles could become Christians without becoming Jews. This was a turning point in the history of Christianity. It meant that non-Jews were accepted as equal Christians. Christianity was free to reach outside Judaism for the first time.

The Christian Church

Summing up

Accepting that Gentiles could become Christians was a major step for the new religion.

Activities

A 1 Why did some Jews think that all followers of Jesus should become Jews first?

2 Explain what the Council of Jerusalem decided. Why was this so important?

B 3 What were the basic rules which non-Jews had to obey if they became Christians? Why do you think these were so important?

4 Write an account of what happened in Joppa, that Peter could have read to the Council of Jerusalem, saying why he believed Gentiles could become Christians.

C 5 Find out more about the creatures that Jews are not allowed to eat. Books on Judaism will have information, and you could look up Leviticus 11 in the Old Testament of the Bible. Write a description – perhaps with a drawing – of the sheet which Peter saw let down from the sky.

15 The life of St Paul

A man small in size, with meeting eyebrows and a rather large nose, bald-headed, bow-legged, strongly built, full of grace; for at times he looked like a man, and at times he had the face of an angel.

Paul was one of the most important people in the early years of Christianity. This description of him was written in the second century CE, whilst people who had known him were probably still alive.

Saul (the name Paul came later) was born in the city of Tarsus, in northern Africa. He was Jewish, and while he was a young man he became well known for his strict beliefs. He was studying at the Jewish University in Jerusalem at the time when Christianity was beginning. When he first heard what the Christians were teaching, he was very angry. He thought that it was totally wrong for anyone to be preaching that someone who had been crucified was God's Messiah. It was impossible!

The killing of Stephen

A Christian called Stephen had been preaching in Jerusalem, and had annoyed the authorities with what he had said. He was brought in front of the Jewish leaders. However, far from saying that he was sorry, he made things worse by telling them of a vision in which he saw Jesus sitting at the right hand of God. The leaders were furious, and Stephen was found guilty of blasphemy. He was dragged out of the city and stoned to death, which was the punishment for blasphemy.

This began a **persecution** of the Christians, and many of them left Jerusalem to escape it.

Saul had been present at the death of Stephen and he decided that it was his duty to try to get rid of all Christians. He learned that some of them had gone to the town of Damascus, and he got permission from the Jewish leaders to go there and arrest as many as he could.

Saul's vision

As Saul travelled to Damascus he had a vision. He saw a blinding light and he fell to the ground. He heard a voice asking, 'Saul, why do you persecute me?' Saul said, 'Who are you, Lord?' and the voice said, 'I am Jesus, whom you persecute.' He was told to go into the city of Damascus, where he would be told what to do. When Saul got up he was unable to see, and the men who were with him had to lead him into the city.

This old mosaic shows Saul escaping from Damascus in a basket

The Christian Church

An ancient entrance to the city of Tarsus (Cleopatra's Gate)

After three days, during which he did not eat or drink, Saul was visited by a Christian called Ananias. Ananias, too, had had a vision in which he was told to go and tell Saul about Christianity. At first he had objected, because he knew how Saul had been persecuting Christians in Jerusalem. But the voice he heard insisted and Ananias did as he was told. He talked to Saul about what the Christians believed and Saul became convinced that they were right. He became a Christian himself, was baptized and was able to see again.

The greatest persecutor of the Christians had now joined them! However, he faced many problems. The Jews in Damascus were furious, and some of them felt so strongly that they plotted to kill him. They put a guard on the city gates, and Saul had to escape from Damascus at night. He hid in a basket and his friends lowered it through an opening in the city wall. Saul returned to Jerusalem, but many of the Christians there refused to accept him at first. They thought that he was only pretending to have become a Christian, and that it was a trick to catch them. Knowing that his life was still in danger, Saul returned to Tarsus, and lived there for several years.

Summing up

Saul changed from being the greatest persecutor of the Christians to being one of the greatest Christian preachers ever.

Activities

A 1 Explain why the Jews were so angry that they wanted to kill Saul.

2 Why do you think the Christians in Jerusalem were so suspicious of Saul?

B 3 What do you think would be the advantages and disadvantages of having Saul as a friend?

4 How do you think Ananias felt when he was told to go to preach to Saul? Why do you think he went?

C 5 What do you think the writer of the description of Paul meant when he said that 'at times he had the face of an angel'? Describe what you think Paul's face might have looked like when this happened.
(**Clue:** What do we mean when we say someone's face 'lit up'?)

16 St Paul's missionary journeys 1

Saul was obviously not a man who did things half-heartedly. He had been a fierce persecutor of the Christians, but once he was convinced that they were right, he became equally devoted to preaching about Jesus. Some of the Jewish leaders were bitterly resentful of this and Saul had to leave Jerusalem, in fear of his life. He spent several years in his home town of Tarsus before a Christian called Barnabas went to meet him there. Together they went to the city of Antioch, where a large Christian community was developing. Luke writes about this in the Acts of the Apostles, but he does not offer any explanation for why these things happened. Saul and Barnabas spent the next year working with the Christians in Antioch, and this seems to have been the time when Saul started to use the Roman form of his name, Paul. This was probably so that he could mix more easily with Gentiles.

Paul spent the rest of his life preaching about Jesus. He travelled all over the Roman Empire, staying in different places, sometimes for a short time, sometimes for several years. He went on four main journeys. The first three are known as the **missionary** journeys. A missionary is someone who travels to another country to tell people about their beliefs.

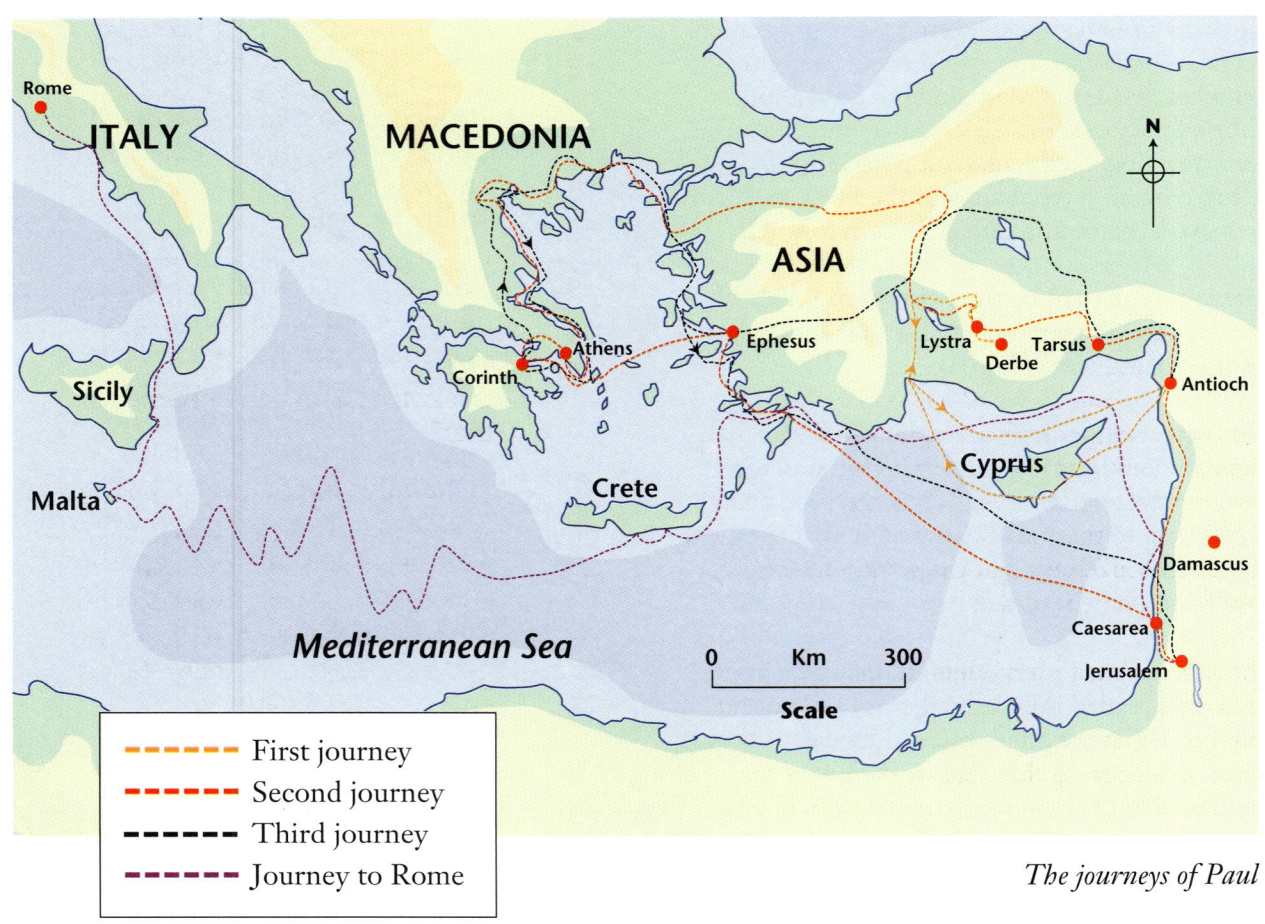

The journeys of Paul

Paul's first missionary journey

Paul went with Barnabas on this journey, which was the shortest of the three. Most of the places they visited were in the area that today is called Turkey. In a place called Lystra they met a man who was lame, and Paul healed him. The people of Lystra believed in the Greek gods. When they saw this miracle they decided that Paul and Barnabas must be gods who had come down to earth. They thought that Barnabas was Zeus, the king of the gods, and Paul was Hermes, the messenger of the gods because he was the one who had done most of the talking.

Paul and Barnabas did not speak the local language, and it took them some time to work out what was happening. Then they spoke to the people in Greek, which everyone understood. They said they were not gods, they were only human beings who had come to teach about the living God. The crowd was very disappointed. Then people arrived from the last town that Paul and Barnabas had visited, saying that they had caused trouble there, too. A riot broke out and stones were thrown at Paul and Barnabas. They were left for dead, but some who had listened to Paul had understood his teaching and rescued them. When Paul and Barnabas had recovered, they travelled on to the next town.

Luke does not give any idea how long this journey took Paul and Barnabas, but he says that they travelled to many places and then returned the way they had come. This was so that they could meet the people who had become Christians on their first visit, and see how they were getting on. They then returned to Antioch, to tell the Christians there what had happened. Luke says that they 'stayed a long time with the believers'.

They then went to Jerusalem, to take part in the discussions called the Council of Jerusalem (see unit 14). What they had to say there was important, because they had worked with the Gentiles. Paul argued very strongly that it was right for Gentiles to be allowed to become Christians without having to become Jews first, and this was what the Council decided.

The Christian Church

Summing up

Paul and Barnabas were the first people to preach about Christianity to large numbers of Gentiles.

Activities

A
1. Why do you think Saul went back to Tarsus? Why do you think Barnabas went to meet him there?

2. Why was the contribution made by Paul and Barnabas to the Council of Jerusalem so important?

B
3. Explain why Paul and Barnabas would have wanted to go back to places they had already visited. How do you think they would have felt when they returned to Lystra?

4. Some people think that the name Barnabas was a nickname. It means 'son of encouragement'. What sort of a person do you think he was to earn a name like that?

C
5. The priest at the temple of Zeus in Lystra was getting ready to welcome the gods who had come to visit them. How do you think he felt when he discovered that they were only men? Talk about it with a partner.

17 St Paul's missionary journeys 2

The second missionary journey

On the second journey, Paul went with a friend called Silas. They travelled around Asia Minor – the area today called eastern Turkey. Then they based themselves in the city of Corinth in Greece, where Paul worked as a tent-maker (Acts 18, 3) and preached. At first he talked to Jews, but they did not accept his teaching, so Paul set up his headquarters in a house next door to the **synagogue**. He stayed there for about eighteen months, preaching and teaching. Then he returned to Jerusalem, which was still the centre of Christianity, to tell the Christian leaders there what had been happening.

The third missionary journey

When he set out on his next journey, Paul revisited some of the places he had been to before. Then he went on to Ephesus, which was a centre of worship for the Greek goddess Artemis. There were many silversmiths there who made statues of Artemis, to sell to tourists and to people who had come to worship her. These men were not happy when they heard Paul preaching to people and telling them that 'man-made gods are not gods at all'. There was a riot, and two of Paul's friends were grabbed by the crowd. Paul wanted to go and talk to the people, but friends persuaded him that he would be killed if he was seen. At last, after the crowd had spent two hours chanting 'Great is Artemis of the Ephesians', the town clerk managed to restore order and things calmed down. This was the end of any useful work which Paul could do in Ephesus for a time, and he left soon afterwards, travelling through Macedonia (Greece) again before returning to Jerusalem.

A statue of Artemis

The journey to Rome

While he was in Jerusalem, Paul went to the Temple. This was the most important place of Jewish worship and Gentiles were not allowed inside it. There were large signs threatening death to any Gentile who entered. Some Jews had seen Paul in the city with a Gentile friend and they jumped to the conclusion that he had taken the friend into the Temple. Although this was not true, it was enough to cause trouble and Paul was in danger of being killed by the crowd. He was rescued by Roman soldiers and placed under arrest for his own safety. This then left the Romans with a problem – Paul was a Roman citizen, and so he had certain rights. They could not keep him under arrest but, with a plot against his life, they could not let him go, because they were responsible for his safety. After many months of debate, Paul solved the problem by asking to be sent to Rome so that he could appeal to the Roman Emperor. As a citizen, this was his right.

The remains of the amphitheatre in Ephesus, where the rioting crowd gathered

The Christian Church

Paul had a difficult journey to Rome. After they left Crete, the boat was swept along by a storm, and they were shipwrecked on the island of Malta. Once in Rome, he was kept under 'house-arrest' for two years. He spent the time preaching to visitors to the house and writing letters. This is where the story in the Book of Acts finishes, and no one really knows what happened to Paul. There is a tradition that he was killed in the persecution of Christians by the Roman emperor Nero in 64 CE. As a Roman citizen, he could not have been crucified, so he was probably beheaded.

> *Five times I was given the thirty-nine lashes by the Jews; three times I was whipped by the Romans; and once I was stoned. I have been in three shipwrecks, and once I spent twenty-four hours in the water. In my many travels I have been in danger from floods and from robbers, in danger from fellow-Jews and from Gentiles; there have been dangers in the cities, dangers in the wilds, dangers on the high seas, and dangers from false friends.*
>
> (II Corinthians 11, 24–27)

The Appian Way – the route that St Paul would have taken into Rome

Summing up

Paul felt that all the difficulties in his life were worthwhile, because preaching about Jesus was so important to him.

Activities

A 1 Why were the silversmiths angry with Paul's preaching?

2 What reasons can you think of why Roman citizens could not be crucified?

B 3 Paul started and finished all his journeys in Jerusalem. Why do you think he did this?

4 Why might the crowd have been so angry when they thought that Paul had taken a Gentile into the Temple?

C 5 What does Paul's summary of his life tell you about being a Christian? Working in small groups, think of as many examples as you can of people today who go through difficult times because of something they believe in.

18   St Paul's letters

In the New Testament, there are ten letters which were written by Paul and three more that may have been by him. They were written to friends he had made in the cities where he had preached, and many of them include personal messages. For example, in a letter to Timothy, he says, 'Do your best to come to me soon ... When you come, bring my coat that I left in Troas with Carpus; bring the books too, and especially the ones made of parchment.' (II Timothy 4, 9, 13). Passages like these help to remind readers today that the letters were written by someone just like themselves.

However, the messages to friends are not the reason why Paul's letters were kept and treasured by the people who received them. For those people, they had a special authority because they were written by the person who had told them the message of Christianity. Christians today believe the letters are important because they contain ideas about Christianity which matter to all Christians, whenever and wherever they live.

In some parts of the letters, Paul teaches and gives advice. In other places, he responds to problems and difficulties that the people were having. This section looks at two passages from the letters.

The importance of love

The passage below is probably the best known of all Paul's work. He was writing to his friends in Corinth, and gave them a long explanation about the 'gifts' (good things) which the Holy Spirit gives to people who follow Jesus. The most important of these gifts, he said, is the ability to love.

The Temple of Apollo in Corinth was already 500 years old when Paul was there

I may be able to speak the languages of men and even of angels, but if I have no love, my speech is no more than a noisy gong or a clanging bell. I may have the gift of inspired preaching; I may have all knowledge and understand all secrets; I may have all the faith needed to move mountains – but if I have no love, I am nothing. I may give away everything I have, and even give up my body to be burnt – but if I have no love, this does me no good.

Love is patient and kind; it is not jealous or conceited or proud; love is not ill-mannered or selfish or irritable; love does not keep a record of wrongs; love is not happy with evil, but is happy with the truth. Love never gives up; and its faith, hope and patience never fail.

(I Corinthians 13, 1–7)

Lessons on how to live as a Christian

There are several places in Paul's letters where he encourages his friends to do their best because everybody has a job to do, and all those jobs are valuable. In this passage, he reminds them to make the most of what God has given them.

> We have many parts in the one body, and all these parts have different functions. In the same way, though we are many, we are one body in union with Christ, and we are all joined to each other as different parts of one body. So we are to use our different gifts in accordance with the grace that God has given us. If our gift is to speak God's message, we should do it according to the faith that we have; if it is to serve, we should serve; if it is to teach, we should teach; if it is to encourage others, we should do so. Whoever shares with others should do it generously; whoever has authority should work hard; whoever shows kindness to others should do it cheerfully.
>
> Love must be completely sincere. Hate what is evil, hold on to what is good. Love one another warmly as Christian brothers, and be eager to show respect for one another. Work hard and do not be lazy. Serve the Lord with a heart full of devotion. Let your hope keep you joyful, be patient in your troubles, and pray at all times. Share your belongings with your needy fellow-Christians, and open your homes to strangers.
>
> (Romans 12, 4–13)

The Bible

XP (Chi Rho) are the first letters of Christ in Greek. This is one of the oldest symbols of Christianity

Summing up

Christians value Paul's letters because they believe they contain useful advice for all followers of Jesus.

Activities

A
1. Why did the people who received Paul's letters think they were so important?

2. Why do you think Paul's letters were included in the Bible when it was put together?

B
3. Where does Paul say the ability to love comes from? According to Paul, why is love so important?

4. In your own words, summarize Paul's teaching about how Christians should live. What do you think the world would be like if everybody really lived like this?

C
5. Paul told his friends in Rome to 'open your homes to strangers'. Why do you think he told them to do this? Do you think it is good advice? What might the advantages and disadvantages be? What would a Christian's attitude be?

19 The authority of the Bible

When was the Bible written?

The oldest parts of the Bible are the books of the Old Testament, which are also part of the Jewish holy books. They were written down over a very long period of time. The earliest probably dates from about 1000 years before the birth of Jesus, and the latest about 200 years after the time of Jesus. The books of the New Testament were written during the first century CE.

Who wrote the Bible?

The Bible was written down by many different men and perhaps some women. Although there are names attached to many of the books, very little is known about most of the people who actually did the writing. Christians believe that what is important is that all the writers were inspired by God.

The Isaiah scroll, from the Dead Sea Scrolls – most of these scrolls are about 1000 years older than any manuscripts known before

Why is the Bible important?

Christians believe that the Bible is not an ordinary book, which is why they often call it the Holy Bible. They believe it is important because it was inspired by God. There are some differences in what Christians believe this means. Some believe that the actual words are important, because they came directly from God. They believe that what the Bible says is literally true. Other Christians believe that the Bible is important because its writers were close to God, and so they were able to put ideas that came from God into words. This obviously means that the actual words are less important. These Christians would say that not all the Bible is actually fact. For example, they would argue that some Bible stories teach important lessons about God or about life but do not have to be believed as something that really happened. The story of the Creation is a good example of this.

How do Christians use the Bible?

> *'And on the day called Sunday there is a meeting in one place of those who live in cities or the country, and the memoirs of the apostles or the writings of the prophets are read as long as time permits.'*

These words are the earliest known description of Christian worship. They come from a writer called Justin, who lived in the middle of the second century CE. They show that from the beginning of Christianity, the Bible has been a central part of worship. Today, it is almost always read in church services, and the **sermon** (special talk given by the priest or minister) often uses Bible teaching, with explanations about how and why the teaching matters in the lives of the people.

Many churches use a **lectionary**. This is a book which lists readings from the Bible, with different passages chosen for each Sunday in the year. It helps to make sure that everyone worshipping at the church gets to know different parts of the Bible.

As well as hearing it read in church, most Christians study the Bible themselves. They read it on their own, and try to get to know it. Many believers try to set aside a few minutes every day for a period of Bible study, and they may meet other Christians for Bible study groups. Someone reads a passage and the people in the group think or **meditate** about it and discuss what it means. Christians believe that discussing the Bible like this is important because it helps them to understand it, and to see how the teachings of the Bible can be used in modern living.

Although the Bible has been translated into all the most important languages in the world, some people choose to learn and study Greek and Hebrew, the languages in which it was first written. They believe that reading the original words, rather than how a translator has interpreted them, means that they can gain a deeper understanding of what the writers meant.

Bible study groups are important for many Christians

The Bible

Summing up

Christians believe that the Bible was inspired by God, and so is the most important book they can study.

Activities

A

1. Explain the different views that Christians have about how the Bible came to be written. What do you think?

2. Why do you think Christians find it helpful to meet in Bible study groups?

B

3. Explain why some Christians go to the effort of learning Greek and Hebrew so that they can read the Bible in the language in which it was written. What does this tell you about their attitude to the Bible?

4. Why do some churches use a lectionary? What advantages might it have? What disadvantages can you think of?

C

5. Use the library to find out about the discoveries made at Qumran in 1947. Work in groups on a project called The Dead Sea Scrolls. Explain what the Scrolls are, how they were found and why they are so important. Don't forget to include illustrations!

20 The Gospels

There are four Gospels. To Christians, they are the most important books of the Bible. They contain nearly all the information that is known about the life of Jesus, and almost all of his teaching. The word gospel comes from the Old English word *godspell*, which means good news. The writers believed that what they were writing was good news because it told the story of Jesus' life, death and Resurrection. For Christians, it is the life and death of Jesus that put human beings back in the right relationship with God.

Who wrote the Gospels?

The titles of the Gospels each start with 'The Gospel according to ...'. The names they give are Matthew, Mark, Luke and John. Very little is known about the people behind the names, however. Matthew and John were two of Jesus' twelve disciples, and for a long time people thought that these were the men who wrote these two Gospels. Experts now think that this is unlikely. In those days, it was not unusual for writers of books like the Gospels to use the name of a more important follower.

This painting of Mark holding his Gospel dates from about 800 CE

The cover of the Sion Gospels, which date from 1000 CE

Today this would be thought to be dishonest, but at that time everyone understood it, and it was not thought to be at all wrong.

A little more is known about Mark and Luke. Mark was probably the John Mark who is mentioned in the Gospels, and who went with Paul on the first missionary journey. Luke's Gospel was written by the same person who wrote the Acts of the Apostles, which begins 'In my first book I wrote about all the things that Jesus did ...'. Luke was also a friend of Paul's and was with him for part of the second and third missionary journeys.

The Gospels of Matthew, Mark and Luke include many of the same stories and look at the life of Jesus in a similar way. (The next unit looks at them in more detail.) The fourth Gospel, John's, is quite different.

Why is John's Gospel so different from the others?

John tells very little about the life of Jesus, and he does not include many of Jesus' parables. His Gospel has lots of symbols, and uses titles for Jesus such as 'the Word', 'light of the world' and 'bread of life'. He puts Jesus' teaching in a different way, too. Important events are followed by long passages of teaching which are called **discourses**. For example, the story about Jesus feeding 5000 people is connected to the passage in which Jesus talks about himself as 'the bread of life'.

Why are the Gospels not all the same?

The Gospels were written at different times. Most experts now believe that Mark's Gospel came first, and was written between 65 and 70 CE. John's Gospel was probably the last to be written, and was probably completed by about 110 CE. The Gospel writers had all talked to different people and used different sources for what they were writing. Each of them had their own interests, and they were writing for different audiences, so they chose carefully what they wanted to include. It would be very odd if four men writing in different places and up to 40 years apart had all completed Gospels which were exactly the same.

This famous painting by Holman Hunt shows Jesus as 'The Light of the World'

The Bible

Summing up

The Gospel writers wanted to show why they believed that the life, death and Resurrection of Jesus were 'good news' for human beings.

Activities

A 1 Why do Christians call the accounts of Jesus' life Gospels?

2 List as many reasons as you can why John's Gospel is different from the other three.

B 3 Why do you think the writers of the Gospels might have given someone else's name to their work? Why would people today think that this was wrong?

4 The writer Mark Twain once wrote that he did not understand why people said they were bothered by parts of the Bible they did not understand. He found he was most bothered by the parts he did understand. What do you think he meant?

C 5 Working in groups of four, think of an activity that you could do together. You could choose part of the school day, or going somewhere together. Afterwards, each write an account of what you did, without comparing notes with the others. Compare the four accounts. What does this tell you about the way the Gospels were written?

21 The Synoptic Gospels

The first three Gospels are quite similar in the way they look at the life of Jesus, and in some of the stories they tell. They are called the **Synoptic** Gospels. The word synoptic comes from Greek words which mean same view. The fact that they are similar does not mean that they are all the same, however. Each of them includes different stories and teachings of Jesus, and reflects the interests of the person who wrote it and the people they were writing for. Mark's Gospel, for example, was probably written for Gentiles, because it contains very little about the Old Testament, the Jewish holy books, which Gentiles would not have known.

Mark's Gospel

Most experts now think that Mark's Gospel was written first. They have worked this out both by studying the Gospel itself, and by the fact that parts of Matthew and Luke seem to copy Mark. (When the Gospels were being written, this would not have been thought wrong.) Mark's Gospel is the shortest, and it does not have anything about the birth of Jesus. Its first story is the baptism of Jesus by John the Baptist.

The Gospel is carefully written so that it is in neat sections which can be understood or read on their own – none of them depends on the section before it to make sense. This has made experts think that it was really a collection of the stories and teachings of Jesus. The early Christians must have been passing the stories on to each other, and Mark decided to write them down. No one will ever know why he did this, but it was probably because the people who had known Jesus were getting old, and Mark wanted to write the stories down while there were still people alive who remembered him. Most experts think that the last part of Mark's Gospel comes from a later time than the rest, and the original Gospel ends quite suddenly in the middle of the Resurrection story. This may be because the end of the manuscript was lost at a very early stage.

A page from the Gutenberg Bible, the first Bible to be printed, dating from 1455

Matthew's Gospel

Matthew's Gospel begins by tracing Jesus' ancestors back to Abraham, whom Jews believe was the founder of the Jewish nation, and it contains many quotations from the Jewish Scriptures. Therefore it must have been written for Jewish readers. Some sections of Matthew's Gospel are the same as sections in Mark, and some are the same as parts of Luke. This has led many people who have studied the Bible to think that Matthew knew Mark's Gospel. They also think that there was another collection of Jesus' teaching, which Matthew and Luke both used but Mark did not. Experts call this collection 'Q'. Matthew also includes stories and parables which are not found in any of the other Gospels.

Luke's Gospel

Luke's Gospel was written by somebody who was well educated, and who was very good at organizing the material he used in the Gospel. He was obviously writing for Gentiles. Both the Gospel and the Acts of the Apostles begin like letters, addressed to a man called Theophilus. Theophilus was probably an important Roman, as Luke calls him 'most excellent'. Luke's Gospel has the most detail about the birth and early life of Jesus. Many Christians believe that Luke spoke to Mary, Jesus' mother, when he was writing the Gospel. He also has most details about the way in which Jesus cared about people, especially those who were ill. This shows what Luke was interested in, and fits with the fact that in one of his letters Paul refers to Luke as a doctor. Like Matthew's Gospel, Luke uses material from Mark and from Q, but also uses material which is only in his Gospel.

Saint Matthew writing his Gospel – this painting dates from about 1064 CE

The Bible

Summing up

The Gospels are not complete stories of the life of Jesus. They are collections of stories and teachings which early Christians felt were important.

Activities

A 1 Why are the first three Gospels called the 'Synoptics'?

2 How can we tell that each of the Gospels was written for different groups of people?

B 3 What were the Gospel writers trying to do? Why do you think no one wrote a life story of Jesus?

4 Why do you think Mark might have felt it was important to write down the stories about Jesus whilst there were people alive who remembered him?

C 5 Read the story of the Resurrection in the Synoptic Gospels (Matthew 28, Mark 16 and Luke 24). Draw up a chart showing the ways in which the stories are similar and how they are different. Explain what this shows about the interests of the Gospel writers.

22 The Ten Commandments

The Ten Commandments are in the Old Testament (Exodus 20 and Deuteronomy 5). Jews and Christians believe that they were given by God to Moses, who was an important Jewish leader. They are rules about how to live, and both Jews and Christians believe that they are very important. This unit looks at what Christians believe about the Ten Commandments.

The Ten Commandments are divided into two groups. The first group of four rules is about how God expects people to behave towards him. The second group is about how God expects people to behave towards each other. In the Bible, the Ten Commandments have explanations attached to them, and so they are quite long. The most important parts can be summed up like this:

> *I am the Lord your God. You must not have any other gods but me.*
>
> *You must not make any sort of idol to worship.*
>
> *You must not use God's name carelessly.*
>
> *Remember to keep the **Sabbath** day as a day of rest.*
>
> *Respect your father and mother.*
>
> *You must not murder.*
>
> *You must not commit **adultery**.*
>
> *You must not steal.*
>
> *You must not tell lies about other people.*
>
> *You must not **covet** anything which does not belong to you.*

This stained glass window shows the Ark of the Covenant, where the tablets of the Ten Commandments were stored

The rules about God

The first two commandments go together. At the time of Moses, most people worshipped many gods. There were gods of nature and the world around them. The people made statues, called idols, of the gods and worshipped them. Everyone believed that these gods were real. These two commandments show that God expects a different relationship from people who worship him – he is to be the only God, and no others are to be permitted.

Not using God's name carelessly means that people must avoid using God's name except when they are worshipping him. Most Christians believe that it is enough to avoid using God's name as a swear word.

From the beginning of Christianity, Christians took Sunday (rather than the Jewish Saturday) as being their day of worship, because they believed it was the day when Jesus rose from the dead. The most important regular church services are held on a Sunday, and Christians believe that it is a day that should be different from other days. Some Christians are more strict about this than others.

The rules about other people

Christians believe that the rules in the second group show how God expects people to behave towards each other. They include rules which most people see as being most important in life – that killing, stealing and telling lies about other people are wrong. They also emphasize that respecting other people is important. They say that everyone should respect their parents, and husbands and wives should respect each other by being faithful to one another. The tenth commandment is a first step to keeping some of the others – if you do not envy what people have, stealing becomes less likely. Some Christians would say that lying and adultery become less likely, too.

Christians believe that it is important to respect old people

Summing up

The Ten Commandments include many of the rules that Christians think are the foundation of their faith.

Activities

A 1 In your own words, explain what each of the Ten Commandments means.

2 Many people use God's name when they don't really mean it. Why would Christians think that this was something they should not do?

B 3 If you had to choose one of the Ten Commandments as being most important, which one would it be? Why?

4 An idol is a false god. What sort of idols do you think people might have in their lives today?

C 5 In the past 50 years, the way Sunday is treated in Britain has changed greatly. Do you think it should be a day that is different, or should it be like a second Saturday? Do you think Christians would agree with your answer?

23 Jesus' commandments

> *A teacher of the Law ... came to him with a question: 'Which commandment is the most important of all?' Jesus replied, 'The most important one is this: "Listen Israel! The Lord our God is the only Lord. Love the Lord your God with all your heart, with all your soul, with all your mind, and with all your strength". The second most important commandment is this: "Love your neighbour as you love yourself." There is no other commandment more important than these two.'*
>
> (Mark 12, 28–31)

In slightly different words, the teaching above is found in all three of the Synoptic Gospels. The first part is the opening of the **Shema**, the prayer that Jews use every day. The Shema is in the Book of Deuteronomy. This is one of the Jewish Books of Teaching which also form the first five books of the Old Testament for Christians. The second part comes from the Book of Leviticus, which is also one of the Books of Teaching. Christians believe it is important that Jesus linked these two teachings together, so that loving God and loving other people are the two most important things in life.

A new commandment

In John's Gospel, the teaching is presented slightly differently, but Christians believe that it still shows the same lesson. Jesus says to his disciples:

> *'And now I give you a new commandment: love one another. As I have loved you, so you must love one another. If you have love for one another, then everyone will know that you are my disciples.'*
>
> (John 13, 34–35)

According to John, this teaching was given at the Last Supper. It was thought to be so important that it has given its name to the day when Christians remember the Last Supper being held. In Latin, the word for commandment is *mandatum*, and this is the word from which we get the name for 'Maundy' Thursday, the day before Good Friday, when Jesus died.

A modern painting of the Last Supper

The Bible

How do Christians follow this teaching?

From the beginning of Christianity, Jesus' followers have emphasized that 'loving your neighbour' – looking after other people – is very important. Many Christians feel that it is part of their duty to look after other people. This may be no more than keeping an eye on an elderly neighbour or visiting someone who is lonely or ill. Some Christians take part in voluntary work, helping people who are less fortunate than themselves. A few Christians are able to choose a job which means they can devote most of their life to helping others, for example as a missionary.

There is a poem which comes from the sixteenth century which sums up why Christians choose to do things like this. It was written by a woman who was made a **saint** after she died. She is known as Saint Theresa of Avila.

*Christ has
No body on earth but yours
No hands but yours
No feet but yours.*

*Yours are the eyes
Through which is to look out
Christ's compassion to the world;
Yours are the feet with which he is to go about
Doing good;
Yours are the hands with which
He is to bless men now.*

Caring for others is an important part of Christian teaching

Summing up

Christians believe that loving God and caring for other people are ways of following the teachings of Jesus, and showing that they are his followers.

Activities

A 1 Write down as many ways as you can think of in which Christians can 'love their neighbour'.

2 In your own words, explain what you think Theresa of Avila was saying in this poem.

B 3 A famous Christian teacher once said that the basic rule of Christianity was 'Love God, then do as you like.' What do you think he meant?

4 Use a Bible to look up the parable of the Good Samaritan (Luke 10, 29–37) and the parable of the Sheep and the Goats (Matthew 25, 31–46). Explain how they illustrate the words of Jesus in this unit.

C 5 Find out about a Christian organization which works to help other people. Put together a folder about the work that they do.

24 The saints

Saints have been described as 'holy helpers'. They are people who were particularly close to God when they were alive on earth. Many Christians believe that this means they are still special after they have died. They believe that the saints can act as 'go-betweens' when someone prays to God, and so make it more likely that God will answer their prayer. The proper way of describing this is to say that the saint will **intercede** on their behalf.

Who can become a saint?

In the early days of Christianity, the people who became saints were **martyrs** – men and women who died for their faith. When the Romans were persecuting Christians, thousands of people died in horrible ways because they refused to give up what they believed. These people were respected by the Christians who were left. It became the custom to remember the day on which they died, not as a sad day, but as a time for celebrating, because people believed that it was the beginning of the saint's new life with God.

After Christianity became a legal religion in the Roman Empire, there were fewer martyrs. People who lived holy lives and showed they were close to God began to be honoured, too. This meant that any Christian could become a saint, even if they were not martyred.

How does someone become a saint?

The decision to make a person a saint is called **canonization**. Someone may be suggested because they lived a particularly good life. The suggestion sometimes comes because people begin to report that miracles have happened. These may take place where the body of the person was buried, or at a place that was important to them, or where someone has prayed to the person or seen a vision of them. Before someone can be made a saint, their life is studied in great detail by a group of Church leaders. In the Roman Catholic Church, if the leaders approve of what they find, the **Pope** may make the person a saint. In the Orthodox Churches, the decision is made by a group of bishops. The Anglican Church does not make new saints, but it does respect saints who date from before the time of the **Reformation**. This was the split between the Anglican Church and Roman Catholic Church which happened in the sixteenth century.

The Churches accept that many people who lived very holy lives may not be well known, and this is one reason for the festival of All Saints, which is celebrated on 1 November every year. This festival honours everyone who is a saint, even if they are not known by name.

These paintings of St Paul and St John date from the twelfth century

Although all Churches respect people who have lived in ways that show they were close to God, the Protestant Churches do not give much importance to saints. They feel that there is a danger that people may begin to worship the saints rather than God. They also feel that people should pray directly to God, rather than asking a saint to intercede for them.

Saints' relics

A **relic** is something from the past which people treasure because they believe it is important. Relics from the saints include parts of their body or their bones, clothes they wore or sometimes even the thing that killed them. Especially in the Middle Ages, people travelled long distances to go to pray at the place where a saint's relics were kept. They believed that this made it more likely that their prayer request would be granted. People who make journeys because of their religion are called **pilgrims**.

Living as a Christian

Summing up

Saints are people who lived in a way which showed they were close to God, and who are respected by other Christians.

Activities

A 1 Why do you think early Christians began celebrating the day on which a martyr had died?

2 Explain why the different Churches have different attitudes to saints.

B 3 Martyrs chose death rather than giving up what they believed. List as many reasons as you can why they might have done this.

4 Why do you think the Churches take so much care before they make someone a saint?

C 5 Use a dictionary of saints to find out more about the life of a saint who interests you. Write up what you find out, perhaps with an illustration.

25 Saints in Britain

Saints come from every country in the world where there are Christians. This unit looks at some of the saints connected with Britain.

The patron saints

A patron saint is one who is supposed to have a special interest in a place or a group of people. Many countries have their own patron saint. The four patron saints of the British Isles are St Andrew (Scotland), St David (Wales), St George (England) and St Patrick (Ireland).

Saint Andrew was one of Jesus' first disciples. He is supposed to have been martyred in Greece, but in the eighth century his remains were brought to Scotland. A church was built on the site, and the town around it took the name of the saint, too. The flag of Scotland shows St Andrew's cross, which is an X-shape, rather than the usual †-shape. Saint Andrew is supposed to have been crucified on a cross like this, because he said he was not good enough to die on the same sort of cross as Jesus.

The town of St Davids in Wales was given this name when the saint was buried there when he died in about 601 CE. Very little is known about David's life, except that he was a **monk**, that he became a bishop and that he founded several **monasteries**.

Saint George is supposed to have been a soldier who died in about 303 CE. The most famous story about him is really just a legend – how he killed a dragon which was terrifying

A fourteenth century painting of St George

people. He captured it, and promised to kill it if the people in the town became Christians. They agreed! He killed the dragon and the story says that 15 000 people were baptized. George became the patron saint of England in the time of Richard I (1189–99).

Saint Patrick was born in about 390 CE, probably in Wales. He was captured by Irish pirates while he was a young man, and was a slave for six years. During this time he became a Christian, and after he was released he returned home and trained to be a priest. He became a bishop and spent most of his life working in Ireland. He wrote an autobiography and other books, and some of his writings still survive today.

Every saint has a day on which he or she is especially remembered. St David's day is 1 March, St Patrick's day is 17 March, St George's day is 23 April, St Andrew's day is 30 November.

Saint Alban

Saint Alban was the first British Christian to become a martyr. He lived in the third century CE, and the stories say that he was a soldier at a time when Christians were being persecuted. He gave shelter to a Christian priest who was in hiding from the persecution, and was converted to Christianity by him. When soldiers came to search the house, Alban dressed in the priest's cloak so that the priest could escape. When he was arrested Alban refused to give up his beliefs, and so he was beheaded. A church was built on the site where he was martyred, and the town around it became known as St Albans in his honour. His feast day is 20 June.

These saints and many others who lived or worked in Britain have been honoured for hundreds of years. The place where the relics of a saint are buried is called a **shrine.** Shrines often became places of pilgrimage. The money given by pilgrims visiting the shrines often led to the building of larger and more impressive churches around them.

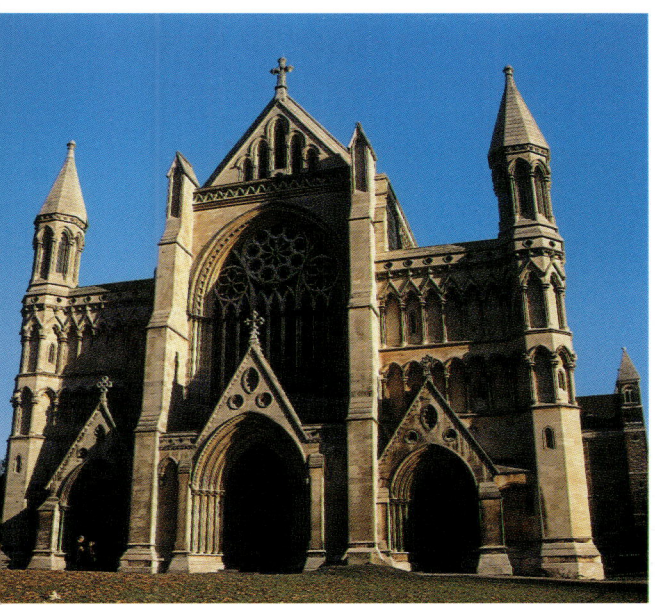

The west front of Saint Alban's Cathedral

Living as a Christian

Summing up

Many saints have played a part in the history of Britain.

Activities

A **1** What does naming a town after a saint who is buried there tell you about what people thought of the saint?

2 Explain why St Andrew is supposed to have been crucified on an X-shaped cross. What do you think about this?

B **3** Why do you think St Alban chose to be arrested so that the priest could escape? How do you think the priest felt?

4 What do you think about pilgrims giving money when they visited a shrine? Do you think their reasons were always good ones? What difficulties might giving money like this cause?

C **5** Find out about a saint who is important in your local area. Put together a wall display about their life and anything else you can find out about them.

26 Pilgrimage

A pilgrim is someone who makes a journey because of their religion. Pilgrimages are made to a place which is believed to be holy. They are part of worship for the pilgrims, who believe that by going on the pilgrimage they will in some way become closer to God.

Why do Christians go on pilgrimages?

Christians go on pilgrimages for different reasons. Many pilgrims believe that going on a pilgrimage and asking forgiveness for their sins at a special, holy place means that their sins are more likely to be forgiven by God. Some Christians go to places which were important in the life of Jesus, because they feel that this will deepen their faith. Sometimes a pilgrim wants to make a special prayer, and hopes that it will be more powerful if it is made at the shrine of a particular saint. Other pilgrims may want to offer thanks to a saint whom they believe has been responsible for a prayer being granted. Others may have their own individual reasons for making the journey. However, all share the belief that the pilgrimage is an important part of their worship.

Places of Christian pilgrimage

There are thousands of places all over the world that are important for Christians. Hundreds of thousands of Christians every year visit Israel so that they can go to Jerusalem, Bethlehem and Galilee and feel that they are in the places that Jesus knew when he was alive on earth. For Roman Catholics, Rome is an important centre of pilgrimage. Saint Peter's **Basilica** in Rome is one of the most important churches in the world, and Christians believe it is built over the place where St Peter was buried after he had been martyred. Attached to St Peter's is the **Vatican**, the palace where the Pope lives and the headquarters of the Roman Catholic Church. For Orthodox Christians, one of the holiest places is Mount Athos in northern Greece. For hundreds of years this mountain has been a centre of worship, and 1500 monks still live there in 20 monasteries. Many important **icons** and other treasures are in the monasteries.

Places of pilgrimage in Britain

Canterbury is the home of the senior archbishop in the Church of England, so the cathedral is the mother church of England. In the Middle Ages, Canterbury was one of the most important places of pilgrimage in Europe. The cathedral at Canterbury was begun in 597 CE, when St Augustine came to Canterbury from Rome. He had been sent by the Pope, Gregory the Great, to convert the English to Christianity. Canterbury became even more important as a place of pilgrimage after the archbishop, Thomas à Becket, was murdered in the cathedral by soldiers of the king. This happened in 1170, after the archbishop had had a disagreement with the king.

This stained glass window in Canterbury Cathedral shows pilgrims on their way to worship there

Living as a Christian

The island of Iona is a peaceful place for pilgrimage

In 1173 the Pope declared that Thomas à Becket was a saint and a martyr and, for 300 years, pilgrims came to worship at the shrine which contained his bones. The shrine was destroyed in 1538, during the Reformation.

Iona

Very different sorts of pilgrimage take place today to the island of Iona, off the coast of Scotland. This island has been thought of as being a holy place for hundreds of years – St Columba lived and died there in the sixth century. After the Reformation, the church there became a ruin, but in the past 50 years it has been rebuilt and now a community of Christians lives there. Over 1000 people, especially teenagers, visit Iona every year and spend time talking and listening to each other, discussing world problems and Christian ways of dealing with them.

Summing up

Pilgrimage to holy places is an important part of worship for many Christians.

Activities

A 1 What is the difference between a pilgrimage and a holiday?

2 Explain why pilgrims believe that their pilgrimage is a special part of worship.

B 3 Why do you think many Christians choose to go on pilgrimages to Israel at Christmas or Easter?

4 Many Christians believe that their worship can sometimes mean more to them if they are in a place where Christians have worshipped for hundreds of years. How does this explain the appeal of places like Iona?

C 5 If you can, talk to someone who has been on a pilgrimage. If it is not possible to do this face to face, find an account in a book. Write a short article about where the person went, and what you feel the pilgrimage meant to them.

27 Inspirational people 1

Mother Teresa

Agnes Gonxha Bojaxhiu was born in 1910. Her family came from Albania, and were living in Macedonia when she was born. Although they were not poor, her father died when she was nine, and the family did not have an easy life. Whilst she was still at school she became sure that God wanted her to work in India. She joined a group of Irish **nuns** called the **Order** of the Sisters of Our Lady of Loreto. After training with them in Ireland she went to India in 1929. Nuns and monks are usually known by a saint's name rather than their given name, and when Agnes became a full member of the Order in 1937, she took the name 'Teresa'.

Mother Teresa's work begins

Mother Teresa became a teacher in Calcutta. The girls she taught came from well-off families, but Mother Teresa came across many people in the city who were homeless and starving. Many were ill, and with no one to give them treatment, they died on the pavement.

On a train to Calcutta on 10 September 1946, Mother Teresa believed she heard God telling her to spend her life working in the slums with people who were poor and dying. She was certain that God wanted her to begin a new order of nuns who would look after these people, but she did not have an easy start. She had no money, she had no accommodation for people, and she had to free herself from the vows that she had taken when she became a member of the Loreto Sisters. (Nuns and monks join their Order for life, and make vows promising this.)

After two years, she was free to begin training as a nurse, and she began working in the slums of Calcutta. For five years she nursed people on the streets, begging for food and medicines to give to them. She began a school for the

Mother Teresa

children in the slums, who were receiving no education. Other women heard about the work she was doing, and some went to work with her. She called them her sisters. When it was approved by the Roman Catholic Church in 1950, the organization became known as the Missionaries of Charity.

The Order's work today

As well as working with people who are homeless and dying, the Order now has schools and children's homes, especially looking after babies who have been abandoned because their parents are too poor to care for them. It runs clinics and homes for people with leprosy, a disease which causes enormous suffering in poor countries where people cannot afford treatment.

Many of the people who are taken in from the streets die, but this does not mean that the sisters feel they have failed. The purpose of their work is to make people feel that they are cared for. Even if someone only lives for a few hours, the sisters say that what is important is that they do not die alone and unloved.

Mother Teresa was criticized by people who did not agree with her. For example, some people felt that rather than concentrating on nursing people who were sick, the Order should try to do more about the causes of their problems. Mother Teresa's answer was that others could do that – it was not what her Order was there for.

She was respected even by people who did not agree with her, and when she died in 1997 she had been given many awards for her work, including the Nobel Peace Prize in 1979. Many people hope that she will be made a saint by the Roman Catholic Church, because they feel that she was such a special person.

Mother Teresa's work for the poor brought her into contact with many famous people

Living as a Christian

Summing up

Mother Teresa was a nun who spent her life caring for other people.

Activities

A **1** Why might nuns and monks take the name of a saint?

2 Why do the sisters believe they have not failed even if someone dies?

B **3** Mother Teresa's first work with children was to open a school. Why do you think she felt this was so important?

4 Mother Teresa said that it was for other people to solve the problems of the poor. What were her reasons for this? Do you agree with her attitude?

C **5** Even people who did not agree with Mother Teresa respected her. Working in small groups, discuss what it was about her that people admired. Write an article about her life and work.

28 Inspirational people 2

Nicky Cruz

Nicky Cruz was born in 1940 on the island of Puerto Rico, in the Caribbean. He was one of seventeen boys and one girl in the family. His parents were spiritualists, who earned their living through witchcraft. Nicky was a wild child. He enjoyed being cruel to living things, especially birds, because he resented the fact that they were free and he felt that he was not.

He ran away from home five times. At last, hoping for a fresh start, his parents sent him to New York to live with an older brother. Nicky started school but got into trouble from the start, and was expelled after he had threatened to kill the head teacher. His brother could not cope with his behaviour and Nicky ran away from there too. He mugged a street trader to get money, and rented a room. He was sixteen and on his own in New York.

Leader of the Mau Maus

At that time, gangs of teenagers ruled the streets of the poorer areas of New York City, and before long Nicky had joined one called the Mau Maus. Within six months of joining, Nicky had become leader of the gang. There were fights with other gangs. Members provided him with drugs, alcohol and girlfriends – on the surface, life was good! When one of his brothers came to see him to beg him to go and live with him, he answered, 'I got 200 boys who do what I tell them ... Even the police are scared of me. Why should I come home with you? The gang's my family.'

In the two years that Nicky Cruz was leader of the Mau Maus, seventeen people were killed in fights between his gang and others. He says, 'We lived as if there was no law.' After one court appearance, he was sent to a psychologist who had spent years working with people like Nicky. After two days' assessment, he concluded that Nicky was a hopeless case. He told him, 'I've never seen a kid as hard, cold and savage as you. Unless you change, you're on a one-way street to jail, the electric chair and hell.'

'Jesus loves you!'

It was about this time that a Christian preacher called David Wilkerson began preaching on the streets of the area where Nicky lived. Nicky heard 'this skinny man' telling groups of lawless teenagers that Jesus loved them. He found the idea scary, and acted tough, swearing and spitting at Wilkerson and threatening to kill him. Wilkerson followed him, telling him that 'Jesus loves you'. Nicky was convinced that no one loved him. He went with the gang to a meeting which Wilkerson was holding, but only because a gang member challenged him with being too 'chicken' to go.

At sixteen, Nicky Cruz was on his own in New York

At that meeting, Wilkerson's preaching caused a total change in Nicky's attitude. 'Nothing else mattered except that I wanted to be a follower of Jesus Christ – whoever he was.'

The following morning, Nicky and 25 of the gang members walked to the police station carrying their new Bibles, and handed in their guns and knives. The police couldn't believe it, and sent for Wilkerson to confirm the story.

In the weeks that followed, Nicky was shot at and stabbed almost fatally by gang members, but he felt that he had a new power. The next year he went to Bible college, and later married a fellow student. He became a preacher and began working with the gangs in New York. With Wilkerson, he began a centre called Teen Challenge, working with drug addicts, especially teenagers. The work was hard, and he said, 'We felt like we were trying to dry up the ocean by dipping at the surf with a teaspoon.' But they believed so strongly in the importance of what they were doing that nothing else mattered.

Nicky now runs his own organization called Outreach for Youth, working with drug addicts and other young people who need help. He also travels all over the world, talking to people about what he believes.

Nicky Cruz

Living as a Christian

Summing up

From being a vicious and lawless teenager, Nicky Cruz became a Christian worker whose life was totally changed.

Activities

A 1   When he was six, Nicky Cruz heard his mother describe him as 'a child of the devil'. What effect do you think this had on him?

    2   Do you think young people today would take notice of Nicky Cruz talking to them? Why?

B 3   Do you think it is possible for people to change suddenly from an evil way of life? What do you think other members of the gang might have felt?

    4   Why do you think Nicky Cruz has spent most of his life working with young people who are drug addicts?

C 5   'Gang leader turned Christian!' Imagine you were a newspaper reporter asked to cover this story. Write up your report.

29 Inspirational people 3

This unit is made up of interviews with two Christians who believe that their faith is the most important part of their life.

Jonathan Edwards

'I can never remember a time when I didn't know God and felt that I had a relationship with him. My parents are committed believers and the reality of their faith strongly influenced me in my own decision to become a Christian. I believe that God created people in his own image, to work with him, but that this relationship is spoiled by our sin, by our not living up to God's standards. Jesus Christ died in order to break down the barrier between man and God, and becoming a Christian is a bit like coming home, because God made us to be his friends.

For me the most important thing about being a Christian is living a life that is worthy of God because of what he's done for me. I believe that men and women were created to glorify God, and so it's important to live in a way which pleases God. Being part of the Church and finding out what God wants for me through reading the Bible is very important – not just on a Sunday, but every day.

My faith comes first in my life, and I don't have any problem being a Christian and being an athlete. When I go out to compete, what's important to me is that I'm using my God-given gift and doing it whole-heartedly. Of course I want to win, but the real question for everything that happens is "Does this honour God?". An athlete trains towards a purpose – to win a medal or break a record. But the medal doesn't last for ever, and the record may be broken again. The reward of living a life that pleases God will last for ever.'

Jonathan Edwards

Jonathan Edwards is an athlete who competes in the triple-jump event. He describes himself as someone who 'jumps into a sand-pit for a living!' He holds the world record for the triple jump (18.29 metres, set in 1995), and has been International Athlete of the Year and BBC Sports Personality of the Year.

Carrie Grant

Carrie Grant is a dancer, TV presenter, singer and song-writer. She has worked with artists like Take That, 911, Gary Barlow and Diana Ross. She presents for satellite TV Christian Channel Europe, and in 1997 released an album with her soul-singing husband, David Grant.

Living as a Christian

'I was born into a home where neither of my parents were Christians. When I was six my parents divorced and I grew up with my mum and brother. I felt quite lonely as a child and the only time I felt really good was when I was performing, singing and dancing. When I left school I became a dancer on TV and then a TV presenter on a show called 'How Dare You!' with Cheryl Baker. I had found success in my work but inside I began to feel the isolation I had felt before as a child.

I searched and studied many beliefs and finally took a look at Christianity. What really struck me was the character of Jesus. He was God, and yet he came down to earth as a human being and lived like us. I felt that here was a person who understood me fully, all my pain and all the good and bad bits about me. Not only that, but he loved me more than any person ever could. I read in the Bible that he longs to have a relationship with us and so at that point I invited him into my life. Obeying the rules and regulations of an angry God would be hard, but Christianity is about pleasing a God who loves me no matter what. Even when I get it wrong!

I work as a singer with top artists, and I perform on TV shows like Top of the Pops, The Smash Hits Awards and Children in Need. The artists I work with know I'm a Christian, and I sometimes chat about it with them. As a Christian I believe that simply being who you are, where you are, has an impact on those around you.'

Carrie Grant

Summing up

Many people feel that what they believe about Jesus makes an important difference to their lives.

Activities

A 1 Why does Jonathan Edwards feel that being a Christian is like coming home?

2 What attracted Carrie Grant to Christianity?

B 3 Why do Christians believe that studying the Bible is so important?

4 Why do you think that many Christians feel they want the people they work with to know about their beliefs?

C 5 Find out about the life of someone who is a Christian – someone you know or someone famous. Put together a brief biography, explaining how their faith has affected their life.

Important places in Christianity

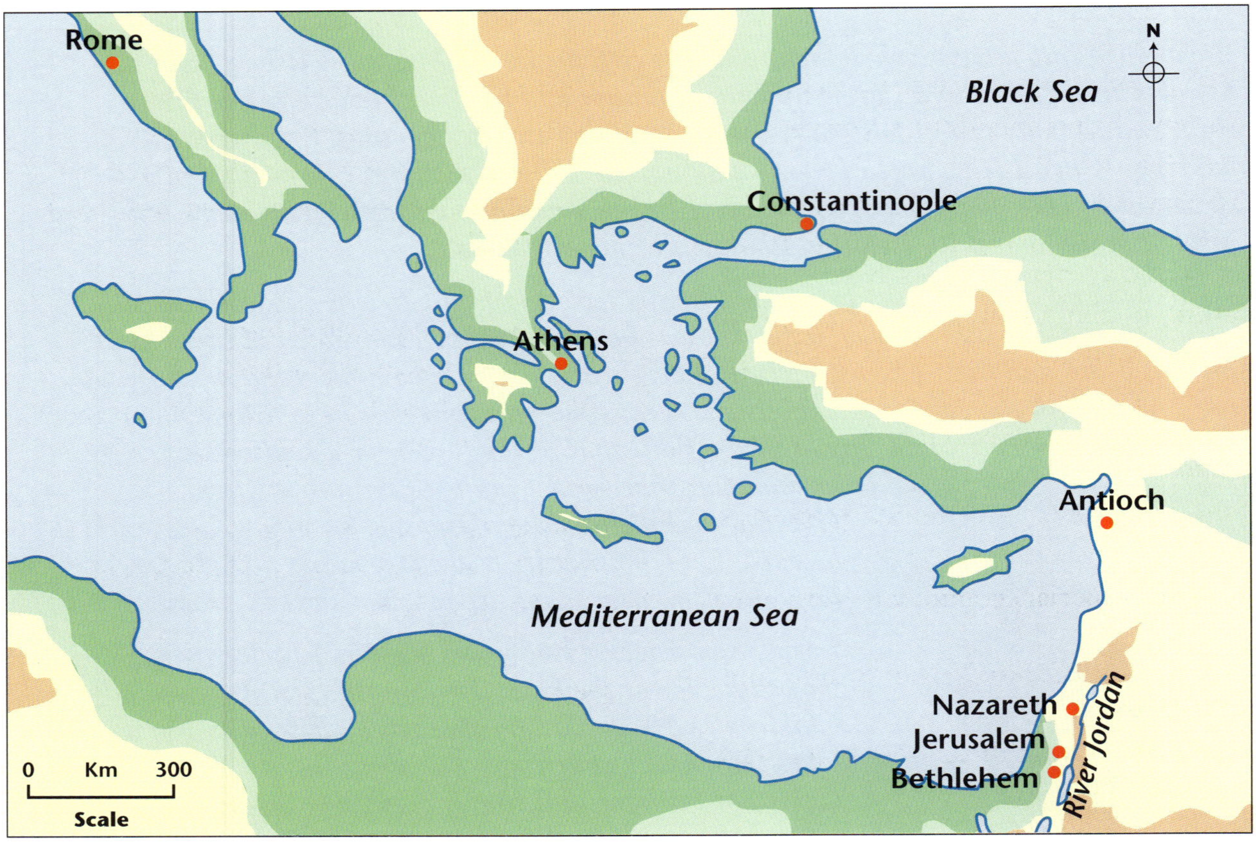

Time chart

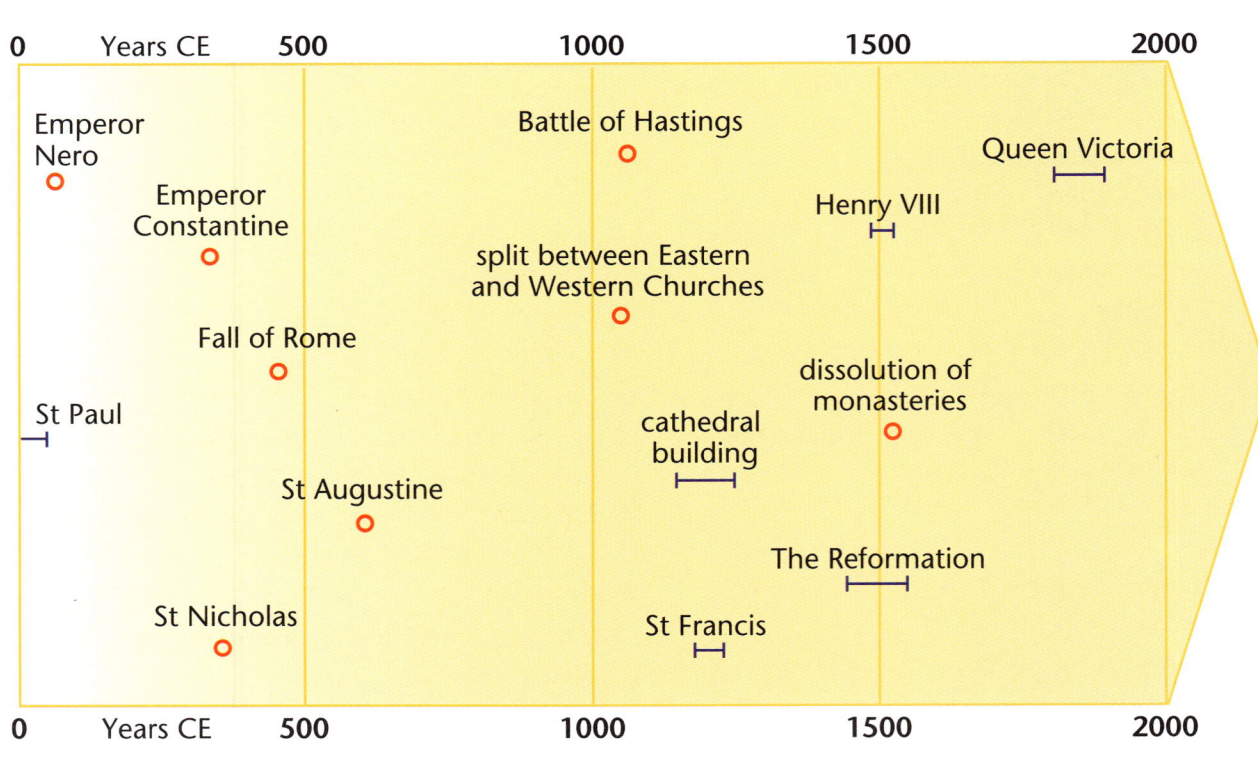

Glossary

Abba 'daddy' (Aramaic word for father)
Adultery being unfaithful to your husband or wife
Anglican the Church of England, and Churches which regard the Church of England as their mother Church
Anoint to pour oil over, or to rub with oil
Apostle 'one who is sent out' – name given to some of the first followers of Jesus
Aramaic language spoken in first-century Palestine
Atonement making up for wrong-doings

Baptism a special ceremony to wash away sin
Basilica type of church (usually large and important)
Blasphemy saying things about God which are not true

Canonization the process of being made a saint
Chalice cup used in the Eucharist
Charismatic Christian worship which emphasizes the gifts of the Holy Spirit
Chrismation ceremony of anointing with oil, which follows a baptism ceremony in Orthodox Churches
Confession admitting the things you have done wrong
Covet envying what other people possess
Creed a statement of belief
Crucifixion method of killing someone by nailing or tying them to a cross and leaving them to die

Disciple 'someone who learns' – follower of Jesus
Discourses long passages of teaching

Eternal without beginning or end
Eucharist special service in which Christians eat bread and drink wine
Evolution belief that the world developed gradually

Fast not eating or drinking for a certain time, for religious reasons
Free Churches Protestant Churches in the UK which are not Anglican

Gentile anyone who is not a Jew
Gospels the four books in the Bible which tell of Jesus' life

Icon a religious painting of Jesus, the Virgin Mary or a saint
Idol false god
Intercede to speak on behalf of
Invocation a prayer asking God for help

Judaism the religion of the Jews

Lectionary book of Bible readings for church services

Martyr someone who dies rather than give up their faith
Meditate think deeply, especially about religion
Messiah one sent by God to free the Jews
Miracle an event that cannot be explained, but which shows God's power
Missionary someone who travels to preach about what they believe
Monastery building where monks live
Monk man who has chosen to dedicate his life to God

Nun woman who has chosen to dedicate her life to God

Order group of nuns or monks who live by the same rules

Ordination ceremony in which a person is made a member of the clergy

Orthodox the eastern Churches, mainly based in Greece and Russia

Parable a story with a meaning

Pentecostal group of Christian Churches whose worship emphasizes the role of the Holy Spirit

Persecution being punished, sometimes for what you believe

Pilgrim someone who makes a journey because of their religion

Pope head of Roman Catholic Church

Protestant a Christian who is neither Orthodox nor Roman Catholic

Reformation the split between the Roman Catholic and Protestant Churches in the sixteenth century

Relic precious remains (usually of a saint)

Repent be sorry for what you have done wrong

Resurrection the Christian belief that Jesus rose from the dead

Roman Catholic a member of the Church that has the Pope as its head

Sabbath the Jewish day of rest and worship (Saturday)

Sacrament way in which some Christians believe they can become especially close to God

Saint someone who was especially close to God when he or she was alive

Salvation Christian belief that Jesus saves human beings from the consequences of their sins

Scriptures holy books

Sermon talk given during church worship by the leader of the service

Shema important Jewish prayer

Shrine holy place

Sin wrong-doing which separates people from God

Symbol something that stands for something else

Synagogue Jewish place of worship

Synoptic 'same view' – name given to the first three Gospels of Mathew, Mark and Luke

Temple the most important building in the Jewish religion

Trinity Christian belief that God is one in three persons

Vatican the palace of the Pope in Rome

Vision dream which includes a religious experience